C4

A
PEACE
POLICY
FOR EUROPE

A
PEACE
POLICY
FOR EUROPE

BY WILLY BRANDT

Vice Chancellor and Foreign Minister
of Germany

Translated by Joel Carmichael

WEIDENFELD AND NICOLSON
5 WINSLEY STREET LONDON WI

Originally published in Germany under the title
Friedenspolitik in Europa by S. Fischer Verlag GmbH,
Frankfurt am Main

© 1968 by S. Fischer Verlag GmbH, Frankfurt am Main

English translation © by Holt, Rinehart and
Winston, Inc.

First published in Great Britain 1969

SBN 297 17771 0

Printed in Great Britain by
Lowe & Brydone (Printers) Ltd., London

CONTENTS

A
PEACE
POLICY
FOR EUROPE

———

1

IN
THE SPIRIT
OF HISTORY

I indicated, when I took over the Foreign Office, something I was very aware of at the time: No one with a sense of history will find it easy to disregard the Great Coalition of Social Democrats and Christian Democrats, nor the fact that a man of my convictions has become the Foreign Minister of Germany.

I am presenting this book not as a man of my party but because of my responsibility as German Foreign Minister. For me this role involves three things:

1   The tradition and the creative determination of a freedom movement whose goal since its inception has been the validation of justice and morality in the coexistence of nations
2   The knowledge that the history of one's own people cannot be evaded but must be borne as a legacy and as experience and that the objective must be to fructify the variegated energies of an indivisible history on behalf of the whole
3   The duty of the day, which I take to mean that foreign policy must not be allowed to become the exclusive prov-

ince of "experts" but must be explained in such a way
that concerned citizens will understand what is at stake:
peace and material existence, freedom and serenity.

The history of Germany is replete with blunders and
missed opportunities involving all social and political fac-
tions. Down to the most recent decades this pernicious fea-
ture of an era has made even those who learned from the
past the scapegoats for mistakes of others.

I see no reason for not expressing myself straightfor-
wardly about the historic personality of Bismarck. It was
history that brought down the German Reich. The demands,
however, for which Social Democracy was vilified as "the
Reich's enemy," have become an integral part of German
reality.

It is scarcely imaginable that a powerful diplomat like
Bismarck—nuanced and many-faceted to the despair of
friend and foe alike, condemned by his conservative class
colleagues because of his lack of ideology—would have
erred in the direction of recklessness or immobility. Such
blunders were reserved for others. The word "dogma" was
alien to his policy; his vocabulary lacked all "doctrine."

"Consistency in politics often becomes erroneous, high-
handed, and arbitrary. One must recast oneself in accordance with the facts, with the state of affairs, with the possibilities; one must take the circumstances into account and
serve one's fatherland in accordance with conditions, not in
accordance with one's own opinions, which are often mere
prejudices."

These words were spoken by Bismarck in January 1871,
shortly after his Reich was founded; it was a statement quite
free of arrogance and bombast; it was sober and modest—
though there really was an occasion for pride. It is a state-

ment that should be pondered, especially in our schools, for it confirms the recognition that a policy of interests does not require unscrupulousness.

In our day national unity can no longer be forged through "blood and iron," even if some fool were to dream of that. Smaller than Prussia of that time and in an utterly transformed European landscape, the Federal Republic of Germany must demonstrate its political maturity by showing if and to what degree it can overcome the attitude stigmatized by Bismarck as one of high-handedness, of all or nothing.

The great chancellor succeeded in bringing about external but not internal unity. The premise of having a state enthroned above its citizens was a misfortune for the evolution of Germany. The Reich, as an agreement among princes, was contrived in such a way that it could have evolved into a democratic constitutional monarchy and become an industrial mass society without any major upheavals if its rulers had really wanted that evolution—but they were unable, and for the most part did not really wish, to bring it about. German liberals showed scant understanding of the working-class movement; they preferred coming to an arrangement with the rulers. Socialists invariably met with conciliatory reactions, but socialism was never understood as a spiritual movement. The universal and free ballot guaranteed in the national constitution was bound to remain a declamatory purple patch as long as the insistence on thoroughgoing democratization was anathematized as seditious.

An autocratic and authoritarian state, its forms delineated in Prussia even more clearly than in the Reich as a whole, wanted to suppress a natural development toward democracy by police methods. This autocratic position had a long-drawn-out life and has not yet entirely died out. In Germany the image of the state as a strict and generally fair-minded paterfamilias has been regarded for far too long as immutable. The persecution of "Reds," the harassment of "Blacks," and the contempt for "intellectuals" were bound to leave behind a trauma pregnant with consequences. Only now is that trauma gradually beginning to disappear, even though on occasion political shortsightedness would like to revive it.

Externally we can be only as strong as we are internally. In his unadorned way the German Social Democrat August Bebel once said that the upward-striving strata of the people were part of the nation and did not want to belong to it merely passively, through mere obedience. He spoke of the "fatherland of love and justice" that was worth being fought for and realized. The distance that separates us from Bismarck's era, and the democratic and social rights that have since become a matter of course, make it plain that the German Reich can be understood only by taking Bismarck and Bebel together.

The poorest son of the people has often been its most faithful. This statement must have often been understood only superficially, as in the allusion to the fact that the Social Democrats did, after all, vote the war credits in the Reichstag on August 4, 1914. In fact, they were more patriotic than a few years later when refusing such credits, because they were being requested not for defense but for conquest. In World War I, those in responsibility thought they could talk on and challenge the world until five minutes to midnight. Instead of putting an end to the murderous confrontations by means of an acceptable negotiated peace, they dreamed of annexations with such blindness that the inevitable happened.

Not only the monarchical form of the state fell; the

Reich itself foundered. Germany was left an impotent, muti-
lated, rudimentary state condemned by the verdict of the
victors and shaken by crises. With immense effort it 'gave
itself a new constitution and attempted to bring it to life.
That effort succeeded for only a short time. Then the forces
of moderation, of reconciliation at home, and of understanding abroad failed and their failure was not only due to enemies within the nation.

No one will reproach me for being among those who
would like to make people forget what our own guilt and
our own weakness or arrogance have meant in our recent
and most recent history. Nevertheless, I must point out that
not only Germany acted while its neighbors merely looked
on. Everywhere, or very nearly everywhere, the terrifying
indications of chauvinism, short-sightedness, and irration-
ality manifested themselves. The democrats in Germany
were not given an easy time of it by countries abroad after
World War I. Too little was given, and too late, when
reasonable men—Friedrich Ebert, Walther Rathenau, Gus-
tav Stresemann—pleaded and insisted. It was not recognized
that their moderate and reasonable demands for Germany
were also in the interest of Europe and peace. Outside
our borders, too, it should not be forgotten that the dictatorship was finally acquiesced in or simply allowed to keep
what it had taken for itself.

It would be irresponsible to use foreign indifference as
an explanation for the whole of the subsequent disaster. Its
roots were embedded in the internal mechanism of the state,
in the spiritual attitude of a society that was not ready to
support that state. Republicans remained a minority in the
German Weimar Republic. The fidelity to the state demonstrated by the democrats—in the postwar turmoil, in the fratri-
cidal struggles of the revolution, and in their patriotic coali-

tions for the salvation of the republic—did not prevent them, these same democrats who had created and borne aloft the youthful state, from becoming scapegoats. Everything was blamed on them—all responsibility for external and internal difficulties, for misery, need, and unemployment. Social renovation was shattered at its very inception. The old forces, in key economic and social positions, had scarcely faltered; in the struggle against Weimar they swiftly found each other once again, propped up and fortified by a civil and military bureaucracy that was in reality sympathetic to the restoration.

On such terrain no self-analysis could grow. On such terrain domestic political hatred grew, the glorification of futile deeds of arms prospered, arrogance luxuriated. The gravediggers of the democracy did not find it too difficult to seize control of a state that was being defended against them merely by an embattled minority. With the Enabling Law in March 1933, when the final period was put down in the death certificate of the Weimar Republic, the Social Democrats became simultaneously the rearguard and the vanguard of the German movement of resistance and freedom.

Yet it is a bitter realization that by some of their own failures, the Social Democrats contributed to their exclusion from government in the Weimar period. And it remains a tragedy that the majority of the people could not be rallied for the defense of the republic against the forces of destruction. Then we Germans proceeded open-eyed through the rule of the brown terror, the horrors of World War II, and the desperation of the total defeat.

Whether we like it or not we must realize that even twenty-five years after the end of the war we still have to bear the consequences of Hitlerism. No one who fails to realize this can forge a wise policy for Germany, and anyone who believes himself capable of managing without an emphatic break with that past will founder. Neo-Nazism is treason to fatherland and nation.

The world has changed since the days of Weimar, but the foreign policy of the Federal Republic is in large part characterized by the principles of Ebert, Rathenau, and Stresemann. Peace, justice, and freedom were the basic principles that they wanted elevated, together with the living energies of the German people. It was through them that Germany was to assume a fitting place in the world and to carry out a reasonable mission in Europe.

With all due concession to the extent of the defeat and the splitting of Germany, German foreign policy cannot and must not disregard the moral heritage of the German resistance either—not to please the former enemies, but for reasons of self-respect; not to preserve contradictions within the German people, but to conduct the reconciliation to a clear-cut conclusion.

The statesmanlike figure of Friedrich Ebert stands out against the hate-laden phrase, the "November criminals." Such men as Julius Leber and Wilhelm Leuschner represent the German resistance against Hitler. And for the self-affirmation since 1945 I nominate Ernst Reuter and Kurt Schumacher. At all times and in all camps there have been Germans to be proud of. As Foreign Minister I am gratified to recall that members of the German foreign service have been engaged in the resistance movement against Hitler. As chairman of the Social Democratic Party I can state that, even in the time of persecution, my political friends have never wavered in their well-understood national solidarity.

The achievements of Konrad Adenauer are esteemed even by those who fought against him. Yet the position of the

Federal Republic on foreign affairs cannot be defined only by the first Federal Chancellor and his colleagues. Others, and Social Democrats not least of all, played an important role when the issue was the reconquest of confidence in Germany.

In 1952, shortly before his death, Schumacher wrote: "What is at issue is giving the German people a new national consciousness, distant equally from the outrageous arrogance of the past and from the inclination, so widespread today, to see in every wish of the Allies a revelation of European thinking. Only a people that asserts itself can become a valued member of a large community." Today, sixteen years later, there is a great deal of talk in our country about the people's need for a new national consciousness. At that time, during the first postwar years, the bearing of Schumacher and Reuter was often mistakenly thought to be nationalistic. Yet it was, rather, an expression of the feeling of integrity, of personal freedom, and of a sense of the destiny of their compatriots. For these men the end of the war was a genuine liberation, out of which they won the strength to make requests in the name of a people whose majority could feel merely defeated. It is now clear how important it was that those who spoke for the people then had unbroken self-respect.

Those to whom I feel politically close, in the narrower sense, were standing up for legitimate German interests at a time when others who later tried to swim along on a nationalist wave were still busy with insincere confessions of guilt or improbable affirmations of innocence. We knew that the guilt of twelve years of disaster could not be wiped out by the evasion of a common responsibility or by a sort of escape from the nation. In the bitterest hours we tried to appeal to the good qualities of our people and to liberate the substantial reserves of common sense that had fortunately survived.

National self-consciousness is different from arrogance and from the overestimation of one's own value with respect to other nations. It rests on a sure judgment of one's own strength, capacity, and virtue—and limitations. To recognize by ourselves the way things are, to know where we stand and where we want to go—that is part of the self-consciousness of a mature people. And that can be a source of healing for the inferiority complex that keeps telling us that we are a misunderstood nation.

Just as Konrad Adenauer's name is bound up with France, with the Western European alliance, and with the Atlantic pact, so the names of Kurt Schumacher and Ernst Reuter stand for political self-assertion—and not only in Berlin— for the assent of the working class to the Federal Republic, for democratic solidarity, and for the campaign to equate democracy and the nation. One is almost tempted to perceive in this a remarkable dialectic that in domestic politics has led to a situation of intertwined fronts. Nevertheless, in spite of world political developments, independent of German politics, and occasionally embittered altercations over foreign policy, the great parties (the Social Democrats and the Christian Democrats) have not wholly drifted away from each other. Our part of Germany had the strength and insight to cross the necessary bridges when, at the end of 1966, there was a question of preserving the essence of the Federal Republic and ensuring it stability and chances for the future in the second phase of the postwar era.

There have been rectifications of the course of foreign policy that can be scrutinized. If nothing had changed, a good deal of the polemics would have been not only superfluous but incomprehensible to boot. No polemics, however, can change the fact that German foreign policy is geared to one common denominator: the ensuring of peace. This principle means, primarily, a European policy aimed at détente, collaboration, and accord.

In all foreign policy matters, then, it is up to us—in a world of explosive technicalization, of a balance of terror, of convulsive political and sociological changes—as a relatively small federal republic, partly to shield the nation and partly to collaborate on behalf of Europe. Anyone looking backward will find that arrogance and a blindness that today appears to us downright incomprehensible have made Germany smaller and smaller. Bismarck's Reich had better premises than the Federal Republic for the attainment of the goals of reason, but the weight of Germany would, to be sure, have diminished even if there had been no Hitler. The war that was begun and lost by the nationalist devastators and their betrayal of Europe and of German unity have made us lose, in addition, something that can only partially be compensated for by economic strength.

Firmness in the representation of our interests and principles can help us to conserve both what has been maintained and the results of the reconstruction. But to help rebuild Europe and to determine its own destiny within the framework of a European peace order, what our nation requires above all is a sure eye for proportion.

2
AT
THE HEART
OF EUROPE

German foreign policy today bears not only the burden of the second lost war and not only the burden of the Hitler regime. It bears still another burden: the mistrust of many people in countries abroad as to the authenticity of our desire for reconciliation and as to whether the democrats in Germany are strong enough to assert themselves and implement their desire for reconciliation. At stake, accordingly, there is also the burden cf the loss or disappointment of confidence.

One can ask whether or not the Federal Republic of Germany has offered numerous proofs, during the past two decades, of its reliability as a partner and of its solidity as a peaceful democracy. I would answer this question affirmatively. But we also should not deceive ourselves with respect to the fact—whether it seems justified to us or not—that the supporting layer of confidence is still thin. Only by acknowledging the lingering suspicions can we understand the excitement evoked by the appearance of a not very impressive party of the radical right. What some people overlook is that democracy in Germany has put forth strong roots and that we are strong enough to protect those roots.

There are three major restrictions that set limits to German foreign policy: the relatively modest role of the Federal Republic in the play of world political forces, the unsolved question of German self-determination, and the above-mentioned, still prevalent deficit in confidence. But there are possibilities inherent even in restrictions.

Even if Germany has slipped out of the true play of world politics, its geographical location at the heart of Europe continues to give it a key position for the future shape of this continent which will still have important tasks to fulfill in the world. Certainly no general European rapprochement will be accomplished without the inclusion of Germany: it will have to take Germany in, or it will not take place. If we keep this in mind, it will not be difficult for us to accept present-day hardships and hostilities with composure. They cannot be of long duration if the peoples of Europe seriously wish to achieve a peaceful future. And what, after all, can they wish for except a future secured by peace?

If we glance about us, we cannot fail to perceive that the present-day situation in Central Europe is the result of World War II. What has happened cannot be undone. I say this to those of us here at home who once again believe that and to those abroad who still cannot or will not forget.

In this century Germany has lost two world wars, for which she was either partially or very largely solely responsible. Thoughtful and responsible governments could have avoided both wars. If World War II had been aimed only at revising the results of World War I, that goal would have been frightful enough. The remote historian, however, might have regarded it as an event that although deplorable, to be sure, was no more than one of the many armed collisions in which the history of mankind is so rich.

We know, and will do well never to forget, that this second war was undertaken for the perpetration of criminal actions for which there are no parallels in the modern age. Murderous acts of scarcely conceivable proportions have besmirched the name of Germany throughout the world. The lacerated Germany of today, which seeks peace and has the honest resolution to build a purified national life, is for this reason still thrust back onto the moral defensive. We must cherish no illusions on this score.

Most nations are like most people in that their memory is sharper about others than about themselves except when pleasant memories are involved. Our nation is no exception. We are loath to recall the defeats, the bitter need, the good intentions, the wretched forlorn hopes. If we visualize the social upheavals, political chaos, radicalism, and hatred after World War I, then the development since World War II must appear to us a miracle; above all the fact that with all the millions of refugees and deportees—a massive factor of potential despair—a democratic state could grow up at all. The world has not taken enough cognizance of this authentic German miracle. The unprecedented extent of the fall, the later subsequent threats, and the concrete form of the division were, to be sure, no seedbed for radical nationalism, which has on occasion manifested itself but has never developed in a threatening form. Moreover, at first there was no German foreign policy at all, and later there was only a very restricted one. Even today, after all, the sovereignty of the Federal Republic is far from complete.

In its inner mechanism, in its economic potential, and in its life force the Federal Republic of Germany is stronger than the Weimar Republic was. At the same time, nevertheless, everything is more difficult today. The war has been over for a long time, but the peace cannot be won unless

Europe is created and the account for Hitler's war settled. This account is still outstanding. We have had to make partial payments on it, and we are quite unwilling to regard all of them as mere installments. But we should not deceive ourselves. When the day of reckoning comes, what will be demanded of us will hardly be smaller than the payments we have already made. The road we have put behind us seems simple and almost all too straight in comparison with that which lies ahead of us.

It will not belittle the labor and the achievements of our people if I say that without the splitting of Europe and of our people we would not be what we are. This holds true positively as well as negatively. The path must still be found that will lead Germany to a secure place within Europe and that will deal justly with its legitimate interests. What is needed is a vision of a Germany without megalomania, a Germany that will prove itself through significant peaceful achievements. What is necessary is a lucid and firm foreign policy, a policy that will be as firm as our inner strength permits and come to terms with the results of history.

If we glance back over the last fifty or so years in Germany, we are bound to take fright: there has been an infinity of mishandling; people have suffered and been destroyed; others of talent and ability, industry, and intelligence allowed themselves to be corrupted; minds and morals have been hit by dreadful ravages. In 1945 there were a great many people who were stricken to the heart by this recognition, but it was only with this knowledge that a new beginning could be dared, a beginning that consisted of being restricted to necessities, in order to overcome the crippling of the moral shock.

Today we are removed from 1945 by more than those infamous "thousand years." And, if we want to be frank,

let us admit that there is still a shortage of a sense of proportion, an astonishing ability to misconceive reality, an
enthusiasm in reawakening what is already history, the difficulty of cultivating tradition without becoming its puppet
and of being patriotic with a pride devoid of arrogance. All
these qualities, dangers, and possibilities were not destroyed
in the battles of World War II, nor have they suffered a
heart attack because of the "economic miracle."

The German recovery—why deceive ourselves?—did not
come as a reward for a repentant conversion. It came from
considerations of utility on a world scale and was, at the
same time, the result of the industry and the self-sacrifice
of our people. It was an ascent to economic prosperity and
to the political stability based on that, an ascent to a relative
ability at dealing with foreign affairs, and an ascent to
industrial power—this time with peaceful means—that could
cast its effects abroad in the world. We finally had cause once
again to be proud of something.

But we are not living in the best of all worlds. We do
not have the best of all states. If there were one, it would
at least have to encompass the whole nation. We have not
managed to accomplish the optimum in the way of self-
awareness; we have not become wise. Yet under the weight
of pains that are only half-forgotten we have fought our
way through to a number of basic perceptions that have
given rise to a certainty: insofar as it depends on us, never
again will murder be wrought in the name of Germany,
never again will a dictator be able to blind the people, never
again will a war be waged by Germans or a government
formed that is not elected by the people.

These are guarantees of our state order. For all practical
purposes they are uncontested. Therefore every one of us can
say yes to the state even though in its reality it may still be

some slight distance from its ideal, thinkable conceptions. And what would a people be, indeed, without a goal! It is our goal, and it remains the goal of future generations, to perfect the government of the Germans, for it will prove itself over and over again to be imperfect. Things cannot be going so badly with a people that professes such principles out of conviction. The alleged signals of decay are in reality no more than twitches of a primitive reflex, with which minority groups who for various reasons feel themselves discriminated against discharge their vexation. Germany is changed; it is more polished; it has also become weaker. That goes for its chauvinists, too, who have never known anything but how wars are lost, how you hold out with heroism and composure until five minutes to midnight or even later. But they have never been able to win the war subsequently—neither before nor today. Today as before they make things difficult for common sense, but they also summon forth an alliance of common sense.

Today democracy has the strength to be strong in giving as well as in taking, but it also needs the strength to show our people what is possible and what is not. At the risk of being unpopular, it must be said aloud that the reality we live in, the legacy of the rule of violence and of the lost war, cannot be changed by exhortations. That also goes for our own countrymen, as they have been influenced by the misuse of their traditional virtues, the persistence of the ancient errors, the steep plummeting into revulsion and contempt, and the soothing balm of the economic miracle. It is also a question of being aware of history and of a certain keenness of hearing when the phrase "installment payment," used all too often thoughtlessly, flits through the countryside and when something is labeled "a policy of surrender" that in reality is leading to a European peace order and does not mean to give up the vital interests of our people but something that is barring our path to a secure future.

Almost two-thirds of the people living in the Federal Republic today were born in 1925 or later. They are free of moral guilt and in their majority have an untrammeled view of our situation that the generation of their fathers can summon up only with understandable effort and self-conquest. This demographic factor should not be forgotten, most of all abroad, where an image of Germany is sometimes drawn that has long since failed to fit. No—we are no longer dangerous because of our war lust and our pig-headedness. What is dangerous, though, is the position our nation has gotten into and in which it is being kept by short-sighted political power interests. Getting out of this position by peaceful means will constitute the stern moral test of our people, the true conquest of the past.

Impatience with the course of history is, in any case, altogether out of place. This history of the Federal Republic of Germany is now almost two decades long. In many respects its course has been obligatory. Some things might have been managed otherwise. But it is senseless to wish to go on waging the battles of the past. No one with influence and importance can or wishes to make the political decisions of the elapsed years retroactive. Our starting point is bound to be what is at hand today.

Some people may recall that there was once an Erhard administration. It used to be said that one shouldn't change horses in midstream. But in the autumn of 1966 there was no stream left and no horses; there was only a handful of riders with no direction and no followers in a wilderness whose dangers implied economic depression and interna-

B*

tional isolation. The collapse of a Federal administration in
the autumn of 1966 was not only the failure of a coalition
that was politically incapable of performance but at the
same time the revelation of decisive omissions dating back
to the reconstruction some fifteen years before.

It is not without reason that we have accustomed ourselves to calling this period one of reconstruction. Since
1945 there has indeed been a great deal of work and reconstruction done in Germany. Impressive as this achievement
was, the great opportunity for the construction of a modern
social order was missed. What was characteristic was the
disorderly, wildly luxuriating, goalless, and planless renewal
of old structures that were founded by favoritism. The
opportunity to strive for new regulations and to seek, with
sufficient speed, links with the scientific and technical revolutions slipped by. This sort of largely restorational reconstruction was bound to founder one day, because the old
leaders proved to be fundamentally incapable of perceiving
in time the unviability of old structures, incapable of modernizing society rapidly enough and of shaping it in accordance with the goals of security, justice, and humanity.

To assert the imperfection of our country is not to wait in
fruitless resignation for a day, still far off in the future,
that will bring all Germans the country in which we shall
be able to do everything better. By means of foreign policy
alone we shall not attain that goal, and in speaking of the
state of the nation no one should speak as though he were
capable of separating domestic from foreign policy. In this
decisive epoch in which we must prepare ourselves for the
worldwide confrontations of the coming years and decades,
internal omissions must also be recognized and as far as
possible repaired. The time has come for the dominant po-

litical forces of this country to concert themselves in order
to bring into harmony what can be brought into harmony
only by a broad majority.

The Great Coalition of Social Democrats and Christian
Democrats—as a provisional alliance—applied itself even
in its first year to more tasks, and more important ones,
than other Federal administrations had done throughout
entire legislative periods. If two such large parties join
hands for practical work, they must take the path of reason,
and sometimes the path of compromise. In our situation
some desires are always unfulfilled. To see in an ad hoc
alliance the danger of crippling parliamentary democracy
would be shallow and unjustifiable.

It has been said that the Great Coalition is doomed to
success. So it is, though not in the sense the critics have in
mind when they say this. The whole of the German nation
is doomed to success if it is to survive as a nation and secure
its future. Our task is to strengthen the Federal Republic
of Germany by a properly understood national policy. What I
mean by strength here is not economic strength or even military strength. Economic strength is useful and can lend
effective support to foreign policy, but that alone will not
make policy. And the Federal army is not a factor of
power that could be used by us in the sense of old-fashioned
national politics. Even if it were, anyone who even toyed
with this notion would belong in a lunatic asylum.

No, what I mean by the strength that must grow within
us is the intellectual and moral strength we need in order
to arouse confidence, understanding, and good will. If this
goal is not to remain idle fancifulness, the interests of others
must be understood as accurately as possible, the points of
mutual interest must then be found, and thus the true inter-

ests of our own country will be promoted. Such a policy of
accommodation and of renunciation of force has need of
firm principles, of an integrity that can sometimes be brutal,
of the same speech with all partners, and of the courage
to be unpopular at home.

The United States possesses the potential for carrying on
a war in Southeast Asia, for providing other peoples with
material and technical aid, and at the same time for preparing to land people on the moon. The Soviet Union has
become the second world power; it recently celebrated, with
much self-awareness and immense pomp, the fiftieth anniversary of its revolutionary birth. In the competition for the
conquest of outer space it is neck and neck with America.
Both superpowers command an atomic potential for destruction that can scarcely be grasped by the human imagination, and the smaller powers with atomic combat capacity
remain secondary in comparison. Very probably in the next
decade China will step onto the world political stage as a
third factor of global weight. Taking into account the conjunction of territorial extent, economic resources, technical
dynamics, military ascendancy, and human reserves, no one
with an ounce of common sense could regard the Federal
Republic of Germany as an equal factor in world politics.
Even a reunited Germany, even if it were to become master of
its own decisions, would play merely a modest role in the
future interaction of global forces. No European state in
its present shape constitutes a world power. These are facts
that cannot be changed by references to a historical past of
the nation.

We know the ending of earlier attempts, begun under
less hopeful premises, to secure Germany "world stature."
Today we are carrying on policy for ourselves as a half of
Germany and with a glance at the whole. We suffer from a

division that has been forced on us by world politics but that must also be understood as a consequence of the Hitler war, one we cannot overcome through our own strength alone, however much we might wish to.

In any case, I shall hardly be contradicted if I make the statement that the center of gravity of our tasks lies in Europe. Although we lack the means and the possibilities of influencing world politics in a decisive way, we are not relieved of the responsibility of taking part in everything that is happening in the world even if we cannot stop much of what is happening there or bring about much that would seem to us desirable. These given circumstances are disregarded by a segment of our public, which often demands that the Federal Republic adopt a unilateral position, emit sharp condemnations, or even "take steps" when events occur somewhere in the world that run counter to the ideas of justice and humanity. No one is going to demand that we approve of something that is manifestly bad, but it would be foolish and presumptuous for us to understand our practical foreign policy as a moral seismograph for all world events. Nor, for that matter, is our moral position in the world of such a nature that we might venture to assume the role of ethical umpire.

Walter Rathenau once spoke of a counterweight to the mood of the people, in which a reasonable foreign policy might or sometimes would even have to be expressed. It is not only today, and not only in Germany, that common sense has a difficult time of it. In any case, I should like to say to the people of good will that it is unfortunately not enough to show even good will; it is not enough to know what ought to be or to imagine how it might work; it is too little merely to ascertain that things are not proceeding rapidly enough or broadly enough or clearly enough. An

"ideal" foreign policy without a parliamentary majority
and in contradiction to the consciousness of the population
may be easy to devise, but it is worth nothing because it
cannot be realized.

It happens that there are very many realities that one
must see, realities that are pushing toward a change—and
it would be prudent for our partners in the East and West
to help them change. I shall avoid denying that our partners
can be prudent. But it remains our affair not to overdraw
our own account.

3

PEACE
FIRST
AND FOREMOST

The will to peace and to reconciliation is the primary idea and the foundation stone of our foreign policy. It is on this principle that I became Foreign Minister and Vice Chancellor, and I have kept to it, at home and abroad, at the conference table and in conversations with partners from East and West and from many parts of the world.

To be sure, all foreign policy must directly serve the interests of one's own people. For this reason the first thing I said in Paris in December 1966 was that our interests speak for intimate collaboration and in America two months later that we represent our own interests with awareness— but without arrogance. It is my conviction, however, that there is no longer any national interest that can be separated from the collective responsibility for peace and for the co-operation of nations. The interest of Germany is peace as it never was before in our history, for war would be the end of us.

In December 1966, when a new administration was formed for the Federal Republic of Germany, we thought it of the greatest importance to give vigorous emphasis to our readiness to organize a genuine peace, which is the criterion for our efforts on behalf of European unity and of the healthy development of the Western alliance, as well as for our efforts on behalf of a better relationship with our neighbors in the East and of a relaxation of the situation within Germany.

Before the organization of the new administration at the end of 1966, I, together with my political associates, had stated that what was at stake for our foreign policy was

To deflect the danger of isolation and to stabilize our disturbed relationship with Paris and Washington
To advance European collaboration and unification
To normalize our relations with the Eastern European states
To relax the situation in divided Germany

and, as the sum of these and of other efforts,

To put in high relief the German contribution to the consolidation of peace and of a European peace order.

The linking of German foreign policy to the common denominator of the consolidation of peace means making an active contribution to a secure peace order in Europe. Germany cannot have any interest in letting the conflict between East and West go on, to say nothing of heightening it. Germany has an interest in a détente—for general, European, and national reasons. Here we are in accord not only with our allies—with Washington and Paris, with London and Rome—but with almost everyone. Here we join with the nations and governments of the uncommitted world. Here interests we have in common with the Communist-governed states also come to light in spite of some polemics. This contribution to peace remains our criterion even when the advance is slow or when there are setbacks.

We wish to contribute to this détente—without illusions,

but with tenacity. What that means, in the concrete situation, is not only to promote the European community but at the same time to encourage the process that will allow Western and Eastern Europe to come together again. We quickly passed the initial stage of our new peace policy. The common denominator of our foreign policy has been discussed in the eyes of the world, largely heeded, widely greeted, though to be sure occasionally doubted or even opposed.

I should like to emphasize that not only the allies but also nearly all our partners in the uncommitted world have hailed the goals of our European peace policy and—though in various degrees—displayed a positive attitude toward the policy with respect to Germany that is included in it, as has been confirmed in numerous encounters. In Scandinavia and in Africa, in Tokyo and in Bucharest, from Latin America and from India, we have received many communications of respect and encouragement that have given us the certainty of being on the right path.

Anyone who wishes to vilify our policy of détente and peace and denounce the Federal Republic of Germany as a state lusting after revenge and hostile to peace would be pursuing a policy that was neither convincing nor promising for the future. Such forces run the danger of playing the role themselves that they are imputing to others. Anyone who disregards a hand stretched out in all honesty must be prepared to have it said that he is not promoting a détente but hindering it. At the same time we remain clear in our minds—as was said before—that Germany, even two decades after the end of the war, still has to bear the heavy burden that was imposed on it by unrestrained obfuscation and unscrupulous arrogance.

The obstacles of an apolitical capriciousness and of a

juridical substitute for politics can be eliminated only slowly. Nothing can be achieved with mere polemics and with merely replying in kind to vilification. We have resolved to put an end to all overoptimism and to take the people into our confidence. We do not wish to speak at home in a way that is different from the way we speak abroad—different in London than in Paris, different with Russians than with Americans. Some people were displeased at our setting about making our policy of détente and the ensuring of peace consistently credible, but many in our own country and throughout the world have seen how serious we are about this goal and how active we have become within the framework of our possibilities. I was and am certain that we can achieve progress—in the policy of détente, our European policy, our Eastern policy, and finally, also, our German policy.

Honesty requires the point to be made that what has been achieved in many fields lags behind the unextravagant expectations of December 1966. The relationship between Washington and Moscow vacillated between contact and collision. Crippling influences flowed out of the Vietnam war. The controversy between Washington and Paris was more difficult than had been feared. The prospects for Great Britain's reception in the Common Market were far worse than we had hoped. And the counterpositions that were built up and fortified in East Berlin, Moscow, and Warsaw as a reaction to the initial successes of our peace policy were bound to dampen our optimism. Nevertheless, there was no reason to give our course a new definition. On the contrary, our conviction that in the long run we would be successful with a creative and dynamic peace policy has only been strengthened by the obstacles.

In my work as Foreign Minister I was able to find a link in what I had thought and said in the years before—as a young man in exile in Scandinavia, as the mayor of Berlin, and as the chairman of the Social Democratic Party of Germany. Before the Federal elections of 1965 I was invited by the Evangelical Academy of Tutzing to give an account of my aims. At that time I described foreign policy in our time as consisting of general staffwork for peace. Today, too, I say: Anyone carrying on foreign policy as a function of military strategy remains a captive of the vicious circle of atomic armament. War is no longer an alternative to peace. Foreign policy, as a means of a worldwide security policy, must protect the peace, promote the forces of evolution, and strengthen communication between the peoples in the East and West and between the power blocs.

The West still requires military strength for its self-defense, this was true in 1965 and is true today. But it was and is also true that the West must be ready to risk peace. Military détente is desirable; the elimination of the causes of political tension is better. Only if we succeed in dovetailing the two will decisive progress on the path toward a secure peace be possible. In the long run peace cannot rest on the balance of terror. It must be propped up on common interests that are recognized and desired as such. There is a long road stretching ahead of us toward that goal, and only tentative steps forward have been attempted. The pillars that can support a new edifice are not yet strong enough. For a long time to come peace will remain dependent on the relative balance of destructive forces. But, as John F. Kennedy once said, peace is not a static but a dynamic process.

The nuclear stalemate between the United States and the Soviet Union has not led to an abdication of politics. The opposite is true: since the end of 1962, when the two world powers saw themselves confronted in earnest in the Cuban crisis, world peace has been somewhat more secure, but at the same time world politics has become more complicated. The United States and the Soviet Union have remained very largely decisive powers because of their military and economic potential. Nevertheless, the last third of the twentieth century started off under the sign of neither a Pax Americana nor a Pax Sovietica.

The general concern—that there must be no third world war—has become, explicitly or implicitly, an important element—probably the decisive one—in the relations between the two superpowers. The terrible war in Southeast Asia, which has been going on for years, as well as the dangerous crises in the Middle East have been restricted fundamentally because the responsible men at the levers of power are familiar with the monstrous force of destruction at their disposal. To that extent the nuclear stalemate has a function and can ensure relative security. Up to now, however, there has been no real accommodation of interests between the United States and the Soviet Union. There are regional conflicts, which for the nations affected are portentous enough and which also cannot always be restricted with absolute security. The development of China and the confrontations with it are additional potential sources of peril.

This condition of political tension has given rise, in European and German eyes, to a particular, also "national," interest in peace. A country that would become a wilderness in case of war—regardless of what laws of strategy the inferno would be ruled by—can have no higher goal than to work for the peace of the world: first, because this corresponds to a common interest; and secondly, because now as before there is a prevalent fear of military dangers that might have their start in Germany. We really must not allow ourselves to succumb to any illusions. Some speeches made in Germany have given the impression that we are thinking too much of war and too little of a future of peace that is worth winning. The peaceful and just future that our peoples wish for will not come of itself.

Our foreign policy is in fact directed against no one. We are not concerned with playing a superfluous and exaggerated role in the forefront of the stage. We do not wish to sow discord anywhere. The Federal Republic of Germany has no military ambitions, least of all an atomic ambition. It does not aspire morbidly toward a "place in the sun" that can only too easily turn into a place in the fire. What we are concerned with is this: to contribute to the détente and to ensure peace in the world. But of course we shall represent our own interests with peaceful means wherever it proves necessary.

Many hopes were disappointed after both world wars. Today we know better than before that seeking peace requires the courage not to be deflected by setbacks or disappointments. Such courage and tenacity are demanded by any foreign policy with a hope for the future. As a European and as the German Foreign Minister I see no alternative to a policy that makes the securing of peace the topmost criterion.

The renunciation of force is a logical consequence of our policy of peace. Agreements designed to secure this end can substantially improve the atmosphere in Europe and bring about a lessening of tension. They can improve the prerequisites for the attainment of a peace order in Europe and can also be milestones in drawing both parts of Germany into the process of détente, rapprochement, and collaboration in Europe, instead of shutting them outside. There is no people and no neighboring state that would not benefit from a pacified center of Europe.

Our foreign policy rests on firm principles. As things are, it must be rooted in the Western alliance. It seeks peaceful accommodation and constructive cooperation in Europe, corresponding to the behest of the age and the desires of the nations. It is a policy based on reason; it seeks the proper measure. Germany is an indispensable element in any European accommodation. I say this in what I hope is the correct evaluation of our weight and of our capabilities. We are fitting ourselves into the elemental endeavor to preserve the peace, indeed, to bring it about in other parts of the world, too, and to consolidate it on a worldwide scale. That is our meaning when we say that the will to peace and to the reconciliation of nations is the paramount theme and the foundation of our foreign policy.

4

FIRST
PRIORITY:
EUROPE

There can be no doubt that the European peoples must assume a greater joint responsibility for peace and progress in the world than they have in the past. To do so, they must unite their limited forces; there must be a closer European accord.

In other words, we cannot remain satisfied with what has already been achieved. But we do not wish to underestimate it, either. What has been accomplished during the first two decades since World War II will quite surely not be underestimated historically, particularly the Council of Europe in Strasbourg, which with its Consultative Assembly has performed an important service in the exchange and formation of opinion.

The real political breakthrough is represented by the Community of The Six, which has been encompassed in the Coal and Steel Community since 1952 and in the European Economic Community and Euratom since 1957. The convincing economic success of the EEC and its build-up as a substantial factor in international relations have become a significant Western triumph. In spite of all doubts and risks, progress was made along the path taken by The Six, and its success produced an effect of attraction. Through its progress toward a customs and economic union, the EEC has presented itself as the core of European union.

German policy since the establishment of the Federal Republic and even before has aimed at the economic and political unification of Europe. In spite of the discussion of means and contents, the promotion of the European communities, their elaboration, and their expansion must be considered as a constant of German policy. We strive for the unification of Europe along all the paths that present themselves. That unification, as we see it, lies first of all in the interest of the European peoples that take a direct part in it. Further, it lies in the interest of the partnership with the United States and the cooperation with other parts of the world, not last the emerging countries. One day, we hope, the Soviet Union, too, and the rest of the East will recognize that a Europe unified in this way can be of decisive importance for peace in the world.

The new administration of the Federal Republic of Germany, as I said to the Council of Ministers of the EEC in April 1967, intends to make all possible efforts to attain the goals of the EEC treaty and regards the accord agreed on in the Rome treaty as a fitting form of European unification. In this endeavor it has the complete support of the German parliament. Thus, the administration's position corresponds to public opinion in our country, which, with practically no exceptions, has favored the economic unification of Europe.

In the last few years the EEC has gone such a long way that no member state can reverse it without harming itself. At the same time, this progress means success on the road to the political unification of Europe, for the more the EEC is strengthened and perfected, the more it will effect, through its existence and its dynamism, unification in other fields as well. The balanced development of the Community is so important because the Common Market constitutes a closed-off whole in which each sector affects other sectors. The EEC must not bog down in the status of a customs and agrarian union but should be developed into an economic union and at the same time its external relations should be built up.

In Brussels in April 1967, I made the point—and even today no change need be made—that the three European communities had grown up historically but that their separate continuation was no longer in tune with the times. As I said, they ought to coalesce into a single European community. The fusion of the executive, one had a right to expect, would be the signal for the fusion of the communities, thus facilitating the solution of many of the questions affecting all three communities. The union in administration and the stronger spatial concentration would also be understood and welcomed by the public. Further, I referred to the fact that with the merger of the organs of the communities the decisive phase for the elaboration of a common energy policy for Europe could be introduced, together with the harmonizing of the rights of taxation and the development of a common trade policy, which are indispensable for the construction of the economic union.

The coalescence of the organs of the EEC, the Coal and Steel Community, and Euratom took place in the summer of 1967, following the decision at the end of May by the so-called summit conference in Rome, on the tenth anniversary of the existence of the Rome treaties. In Brussels, accordingly, a joint European commission was formed under the chairmanship of Jean Rey, auguring the departure, after long and valuable service, of Professor Walter Hallstein.

The year 1967 was encouraging in some ways but disappointing in others for the EEC. It witnessed the successful termination of the Kennedy Round, difficult negotiations concerning the lowering of customs tariffs. Of comparable significance were the joint emergence of The Six in the solution of international currency problems and their solidarity vis-à-vis each other and Great Britain in November 1967, when it came to devaluating the pound.

The attempt to expand the EEC, however, as provided for in the Rome treaty and proposed by Great Britain and other European states, was not successful. Franco-German cooperation, also, which had been revived, failed at first in the face of this task, which we shall speak of shortly.

In the beginning of 1967 I stated, in the name of the German Federal government, in Bonn and Paris, in Strasbourg and Brussels, in Rome and London, in the Hague and Copenhagen, that the EEC treaty is open to the entry of all European states. States that wish to enter must, to be sure, agree with the common fundamental concept of the economic and political union of Europe, as well as with the decisions that have since been taken on the basis of the Rome treaty. On the other hand, the accession of new member states will make transition regulations unavoidable. The entry of Great Britain and other European Free Trade Area (EFTA) states would fill in the gap between the two European economic groupings. We cannot take it for granted that such opportunities will be repeated at will. Hence we all bear the responsibility for exploiting the possibility now being offered. The division of Western Europe into two economic groupings must not be allowed to continue. Europe's stance in the world would be substantially stronger if the community were expanded—not only economically and technologically but politically as well.

We had come to the conviction that Great Britain and other EFTA states were earnest in their desire to join the community. Similarly we were of the opinion that the questions of British entry into the community, while surely far from simple, could be solved in an objective way.

An interim balance sheet as of the beginning of 1968 yielded some disappointing results. We still had made no progress in the sought-after expansion of the communities. It is just in this area, however, that I am not one of the pessimists. In any case, I take it as significant that on December 19, 1967, the Council of Ministers established that no one was against expansion in principle and that everyone agreed that the applications for entry were to remain on the agenda.

Nor was any progress achieved in 1967 on behalf of the sought-after political unity. Even the attempt, prompted by the summit conference in Rome, to discuss the possibilities of political collaboration within the circle of foreign ministers remained fruitless. Among other factors, this difficulty is linked to the fact that the French state executive is cool to the idea of any sovereignty above the state. Even independently of that, it has been demonstrated that all those who thought that political integration would evolve more or less automatically out of economic integration were in error. Experience has taught that it is sensible for us to base ourselves on a perspective of intergovernmental cooperation. Qualified political cooperation between governments will not be easy either. But it might mean a great deal. And it would not have to mean that the democratic corrective of parliamentary controls and collaboration would be waived.

In all this the great goal of a United States of Europe should not slip away from us.

Summit conferences—as was shown by the experience of May 1967—are no panacea. Those who take the summits by storm require good form for the ascent, and without appropriate preparations the air of the heights can be dangerous; today Europe is not in its best form for bold mountaineering. I am for a policy that is oriented to imaginative goals and that strives forward but that at the same time remains sober and realistic. We must recognize that a political federation with supranational institutions will not become a reality in the immediate future. As things are, it would not at present be given a shape even among the six countries of the Common Market. In our planning for the future of Europe we ought to cross every traversable stretch of the road in a realistic way. This does not detract at all from the idea of integration, which is just as grandiose a conception today as it was years ago. Nor, for that matter, is it a mere conception any longer, because the EEC already contains, looking beyond the economic factors, partial aspects of political integration that must not be destroyed but further developed.

There is one vexatious burden on the debate concerning Europe that I should like to refer to here. The magnificent debut that remains bound up with the names of Schuman, de Gasperi, and Adenauer was on occasion ideologized in a harmful way. Overzealous interpreters attempted to lend it a partly Carolingian and partly Christian Democratic interpretation. Later there was a question of whether or not this might be counterposed by a Social Democratic ideology of Europe.

Everyone knows where I stand. I am a Social Democrat, but I am against any hard and fast formula which for that reason alone is harmful. What is at issue in reality is for European cooperation to take in all democratic forces. It must not be dependent, in its functioning, on a change of government in one country or another. Leading figures from related political camps can do various things in order to promote European development. They should, however, withstand all forms of ideologization that will weaken instead of strengthen Europe.

In spite of the unsatisfactory state of Western European cooperation I regard it as vital to take a clear look at the overcoming of barriers between the East and the West. I have never conceived of the Western European community as a citadel for us to burrow into and entrench ourselves against the world around us. The Europe of The Six and an expanded Western Europe as well must not stand against its neighbors; it must attract, not repel, them. It must be open, not shut off. Without allowing ourselves to be inhibited by a theoretical dispute over aims, we must move forward to our goal through economic collaboration with the countries of Eastern Europe.

Constructive relations between Western and Eastern Europe are a commandment of our times. For many years I have come out for objective communication with the peoples and governments of the Eastern European states and for the coordination of a policy with respect to Eastern Europe, and I cling to this point in spite of the obvious difficulties.

In May 1964 I said in New York that we must propose joint enterprises to the nations of Eastern Europe and make it clear to them that we are not afraid of the approximation of their standard of living to our own but are willing to help them achieve this goal, a position that corresponds to the original idea behind the Marshall Plan. Independently of political solutions the West should move on to practical projects that are capable of linking Eastern and Western Europe together over and beyond the Iron Curtain.

A few months later I attempted to concretize this proposed goal in a memorandum initially intended for Secretary of State Dean Rusk. In this memorandum I referred among other things to the possibility of activating the

Geneva United Nations Commission for Europe for these
tasks, an idea that was also considered on the Yugoslav and
Polish side. At the time questions were raised in Bonn as to
whether a Berlin mayor was authorized at all to discuss such
questions with the foreign ministers of friendly governments
—a favorite method of evading the substance of something
by quarreling over jurisdictions.

I am eager to emphasize this too: European unification has
never appeared to me a way of setting up a front against
the United States. My opinion was and remains that wherever we Europeans can progress without the United States
we should do so. During the past few years Europe could
have made a beginning in a variety of things without waiting
for the Americans to go ahead. The Americans would not
have been unhappy had there been greater European initiative. We Germans, too, might have done with more initiative
and a wholesome self-interest. But there are problems for
us in Europe that cannot be solved without the cooperation
of the United States and without its support.

The paramount issue is the preservation of peace. Europe
alone cannot defend itself in a worldwide conflict, and I do
not foresee a time when it could. I therefore believe that
there must remain a possibility of acting independently
without committing suicide. My further thought is what a
catastrophe it would be if the idea of a constructive Atlantic
partnership, which John F. Kennedy, with his mixture of
realism and vision, flung into the debate, might not still
become actuality.

For myself, in any case, it remains incontestable that the
peoples of Europe must unite their limited forces in order
to assume a greater joint responsibility for peace and progress in the world. It is because of this that a closer European
accord is necessary.

5

FRANCE-GERMANY: THE PRIMACY OF PROXIMITY

The development of Franco-German relations is of decisive importance for the future of Europe. Without an intimate and trusting relationship between Germany and France no European peace order is thinkable. Europe cannot be built outside France and Germany.

The reconciliation of the French and German peoples is one of the most important realities of the postwar world. It cannot be shaken, nor can anyone in the world maintain that the phenomenon runs counter to anyone's interests. The reconciliation of these two peoples, who have been hostile to each other for centuries, is anchored in the hearts of the younger generation of both countries and therefore is only conditionally dependent on the relationship between the governments. My conviction of this has been strengthened in many ways during the past few years, whenever I have had occasion to express myself on this theme. People have a feeling that an intimate collaboration between the French and Germans in the Europe of the future will be an abiding element in the consolidation of peace. They realize that friendship with our French neighbors must be one of the primary goals, one of the initial tasks, of German foreign policy in the wholesome spirit of German democracy. After everything we have been through, we must, on both sides, take as our starting point the union of our resources. Both here and there everyone knows that such a union is in our own self-interest, as it is in the interest of the preservation of peace and the welfare of other nations.

In the government statement of December 1966 we put forward these considerations with respect to the Franco-German relationship:

1   The facts of European geography and the sum total of the history of our continent have given rise, in the conditions of the present, to a particularly high degree of accord between the interests of our two nations and countries.

2   Together with France, the oldest American ally in Europe, we regard an alliance between the free nations of Europe, now coming together, and the United States of America as indispensable, whatever shape may be taken in the future by the structure of that alliance because of a changing world.

3   Together with France we have come out for the restoration of the historically evolved European family of nations, a goal that encompasses the counterhistorical and unnatural sundering of our own nation.

4   The Franco-German cooperation that we desire is not directed against any other nation or country. It is rather the crystallization point of a policy that has set itself the goal of a unification of Europe. It is indispensable if Europe is to become a jointly responsible partner. That Europe that speaks "with a single voice," as has been demanded by American statesmen, has as a prerequisite a constantly growing concord in German and French

policy. Europe can be built only with France and Germany together, not without and still less against one of the two countries. What is at issue are practical steps on the road to unification, not the unyielding pursuit of ideal conceptions. What is desirable must not hinder what is possible.

5 For the improvement of relations with the Eastern European neighbors Franco-German cooperation in as many areas as possible is of the greatest value.

6 For all these reasons the Federal government wishes to utilize as concretely as possible the opportunities for the coordination of the policies of both countries that are contained in the Franco-German treaty of January 22, 1963.

At the same time reference was made to the fact that the special circumstances of both nations would cast up differences of interests and opinions in a variety of questions in the future, too. Friendship does not mean the neglect of one's own interests or the mere mimicking of what others say. We have often told our French neighbors openly that we have a different view of the question of extending the EEC. We said that in our opinion the time had come to enlarge the community to include Great Britain and other countries that were ready for it and competent. We tried to convince Paris that the enlargement would mean not only an economic but also a political strengthening of Europe. It may be that we have not yet said this distinctly enough. It may be that it has not become clear enough what our own interests make imperative and how anachronistic we consider it to approach questions of European unity by speculating which of the old national states is capable of gaining hegemony.

We have explained that in our opinion a secure alliance

C

with the United States is necessary for the achievement of European security and its guarantee. We said that Europe, in the midst of organizing itself, could not go on existing back to back with America, but only with a readiness for open cooperation across the Atlantic Ocean. General de Gaulle, like others, foresees a time in which the United States neither would nor could remain militarily present in Europe as it was during the first two postwar decades. But whereas French policy is bound to appear as though it were consciously striving for a decisive diminishing of the American presence in Europe, we interpret our own interests differently.

It is our view that Europe cannot renounce an association with the United States. This position would persist—as far as we can see at present—even if a satisfactory European security system were to be developed. Meanwhile, it may become important to strengthen the European component within the Atlantic alliance. Here our hope is that French cooperation within the alliance will be maintained as far as is possible, for a total withdrawal of France would raise very serious questions. Furthermore, a scrutiny of the data of changing world politics would be in the common interest. The joint studies of the world situation and European security in the 1970s, as agreed upon and initiated between Bonn and Paris, may be helpful in that respect.

Recently it was my misfortune to become involved in a distasteful altercation. On February 3, 1968, in Ravensburg I said to my party colleagues from Baden-Württemberg:

Franco-German reconciliation and friendship are deeply rooted in the hearts of people on both sides, and that is a good thing. This holds precisely for the younger generation.

I hope that the anchoring is already so strong that even un-reasonable regimes will no longer be in the position of changing it. The impression must never arise that the motto "Cowardice vis-à-vis one's friend" could ever apply to German policy.

What holds good for Franco-German cooperation is the primacy of neighborliness. Friendly, trustful cooperation does not at all mean that one follows the lead of the other, but rather that one objectively, clearly, and manfully represents what one considers and what one's interests make impera-tive.

Set off by a false report, to the effect that this aimed a personal attack against President de Gaulle, reactions took place in France that I could scarcely understand. If I had had any false illusions, they would have been emphatically dissipated. Thus, I could do no more than reaffirm my con-viction that only if both countries, in spite of some differ-ences of opinion, stand together, only if they constantly try to find a common approach to the great questions, will this Europe, which General de Gaulle is fond of referring to as the cradle of civilization, be anything more than a geographi-cal concept.

I had met the French President many times, beginning when I was the mayor of Berlin. I paid no attention to the black and white images of him that many people had formed. To the annoyance of some people I said as much publicly in New York on May 15, 1964:

> If we recall President Kennedy's vision, which brought so much hope not to my own city alone, it will become clear to us how remote we still are from the great goals. We still do not have a constructive Atlantic partnership. Instead of that we are undergoing signs of crisis in the NATO. And

instead of a free Europe speaking with a single voice, we hear over and over the cacophonies of a strength-dissipating rivalry.

In my opinion it is neither sensible nor fair to make General de Gaulle responsible for all the difficulties we confront in the West. Some of the decisions made by the President of France are not easy to understand, but I have not come to the United States to complain about him. Rather there is cause for us to become aware of the fact that de Gaulle in his own way is thinking of the unthinkable with boldness and independence and has begun to draw conclusions from it.

The equilibrium of terror held in balance by the two superpowers, creates enough free ground to set the congealed fronts in motion. The President of France is making use of this in his own way. And sometimes I ask myself, as a German: "Why, really, should it be he alone?" If we build bridges from the past to the future, it is not obligatory for us to forget the present.

In June 1964 I spoke at the German Society for Foreign Affairs on the interesting experience I had had as a result of the above-mentioned passage in my speech in New York and recalled the truism that in political realities there are positions that cannot be summed up by a simple pro or a simple con. For me, I said, there were three aspects involved when the President of France came up for discussion:

The first is that of immense esteem. Statesmanlike greatness cannot be taken away from this man even by someone who does not agree with many of his decisions. And I believe our people can bear the openness of the considered judgment, which is a good medicine against all thinking in clichés.

The second element concerning de Gaulle lies in the fact

that, from the point of view of the Western community, I regret some of his basic decisions. This holds true for questions of European unification, of the Atlantic partnership, and also of NATO and of nuclear defense. The security of Western Europe is indivisible. It rests ultimately on the trustworthiness of the American commitment. The cement of the alliance is confidence. And anything that might loosen the attachments of the United States to Europe or its interest is bad.

The third element is the fact that de Gaulle in his own way is utilizing the political freedom of movement that has been won by the nuclear stalemate of the world powers. At home in Germany it has often been said: Movement is not good by itself alone. This is of course true. But it is after all no more than one of those catchwords that get one no further. For motionlessness by itself alone is also not a good thing. Especially not when a hard-frozen ice cover breaks up and the ice floes start moving. The name one uses for this event is at bottom not what is decisive. What is decisive is the event itself.

I said that de Gaulle makes use of this situation in his own way. And the question of why he alone should do this is to be understood exactly as it was asked. The Americans and the British make use of the relative freedom of movement in their own way. Other states react similarly. And what do we do? The Federal Republic cannot, of course, play possum. Put less colloquially, it cannot give the appearance of having no interest and no will of its own. Hence the question concerning the use to be made of the possibility of movement can be asked by the Federal Republic, too. But it is, obviously, not a question and not a problem for the Federal Republic only. This is where the sense of

the respectful or friendly warning comes out behind the
question: Why, really, should it be de Gaulle alone?

For me it was no surprise that after the formation of the
new Federal administration there was no difficulty in finding
a thoroughly close accord in those questions touching on
Eastern policy. Here there was not a question of who had
to suit whom but the fact that German as well as French
policy desired a détente and consequently was bound to be
interested in improved relations with the nations and states
of Eastern Europe. Both of us, Paris and Bonn, envisage a
joint European future; in this respect German and French
interests run parallel. Thus, a trustful and productive exchange of opinion in precisely this area was natural.

But the question has also been raised, understandably, as
to why the Franco-German treaty of January 1963 was
unable to lead to far more extensive joint political action.
Here I must say first of all that I was one of those who was
not convinced then that the timing and the form of the treaty
had been pondered well enough. Since then I have come to
the additional insight that the effectiveness of the subsequent
consultations has been uneven. A point will have to be made
of not allowing a grandiose task to turn into mere routine.

At the beginning of 1963 the German side regarded as
necessary a statement of the Federal parliament to make
clear that the Franco-German treaty must not diminish or
even bring into question the other obligations and political
aims of the Federal Republic. This measure of the Federal
parliament secured the assent of the then Social Democratic
opposition to the projected treaty. In fact, such clarification
was also in the interest of France—even though official Paris
took a different view of it—especially because France has
always recognized the special situation of the Federal Re-

public with respect to its need for security and to the division of the country. It was this clarification that excluded any mistaken interpretation of the treaty as being a special alliance at the expense of other vital interests.

The German Social Democrats have committed themselves as formerly, and especially in the Weimar Republic, to friendship with France. After the last war the German Social Democratic Party did everything in its power, when in the parliamentary opposition as well as when a government party, to promote the reconciliation of the two peoples and to strengthen their collaboration. In the great questions of reconciliation and peace it is precisely in this area that there is no party monopoly grounded in the accident of governmental responsibility. Governmental authority has given my political friends and myself abundant opportunity to prove that we are not merely proffering lip service to the unification of Europe and to cooperation with France.

In January 1968, when the Franco-German treaty was five years old, its purpose was bound to be brought into question. We realized quite clearly that the treaty had three different designations. The official title is "Treaty Concerning Franco-German Cooperation." In political usage the designations "friendship treaty" and "consultation pact" have also become common. These wordings undoubtedly merely reflect different aspects of the same political subject. The practical cooperation that is specifically regulated in the treaty is a visible sign of the reconciliation of the two peoples. In accordance with the will of the signers, the treaty sets the seal on their solidarity. To be sure, there would have been no need for this treaty to bring about the historic fact of Franco-German reconciliation and solidarity. For, as I have already tried to indicate, the population and especially the youth of both nations had already directed its gaze to the future. At bottom the governments were merely realizing what people were feeling and thinking.

On the occasion of the signing of the treaty, President de Gaulle and Chancellor Adenauer issued a joint statement, in which they called the cooperation that had been decided upon an indispensable stage on the road to a united Europe. This formulation forestalled the misunderstanding to the effect that behind such cooperation there lay the intention of forming a separate union. The talk of such a union as the kernel of a political community has only done harm to the cause and otherwise not advanced matters.

Nevertheless, the institutionalized cooperation of Germany and France has been anything but a failure. Here I am thinking primarily of the exchange of youth and of cultural links. The picture is not so positive, to be sure, if one takes as a standard the grandiose aims of the signers that, taken together, were to culminate in the formation of a joint policy. But joint action cannot be forced via a mechanism for consultation; it must be achieved through work.

Both governments are committed by the treaty to joint periodical cabinet consultations at relatively brief intervals. The meetings of the heads of the government, of the foreign ministers and departmental ministers, together with subsequent plenary sessions—as a whole all have been fruitful and useful. To be sure, if it had been thought that as a result of such meetings alone a joint policy might come into being, experience has proved this hope to be unwarranted.

The useful instrument of a treaty cannot be made responsible for the blunders and unfortunate developments that have come about during past years, the value of consultation is not thereby lessened. In any case it is important between two neighbors that are so dependent on each other;

but that does not mean that governments must make themselves captives of procedures in the sense that their mere practice becomes the criterion of their relations.

At the first meetings that the Chancellor and I had with President de Gaulle, Prime Minister Pompidou, and Foreign Minister Couve de Murville, a readiness was shown on both sides to fill the treaty of January 1963 with new life. We resolved to intensify our collaboration. Indeed, the economic cooperation between our two countries, including the voting on monetary matters, has made heartening progress. We are striving for further progress in the domains of technology, science, and research and such initial results can be seen, as the joint projects of the Grenoble reactor and the television satellite. Others will follow. There has also been progress in joint plans and in political consultation in the area of developmental aid. In all this it is only natural for us to be also concerned with securing an appropriate economic share for our achievements.

We stand behind the goals of the Franco-German treaty and remain resolved to use this instrument of cooperation and consultation for the good of both countries and for the good of Europe in order to serve peace in the world. As far as we are concerned, the bitter remark General de Gaulle made a few years ago—to the effect that treaties, like young girls and roses, quickly fade—will not come true. We know that a decisive role for the future of Europe is going to devolve on the development of relations between Germany and France.

c*

6

THE
SIX—AND THE
OTHER RELATIVES

Great Britain and the other states that are willing to join must find their place in the Common Market and in the European community. The abyss between the EEC and the EFTA must be filled in.

In December 1966, when forming a new Federal administration, we jointly stated that the Community of The Six ought to stay open to all European states that accepted its aims; we were merely recalling what was already contained in the Rome treaty. We did not offer mere expressions of sympathy for the participation of Great Britain and other EFTA countries but emphasized that we were going to apply ourselves energetically to the extension of the European communities. I have kept to that.

The extension of the EEC is, for us, a common European interest that also corresponds to our own interests in Germany. No one can remain unclear as to what we consider desirable and what we consider possible. But at the same time we have to be clear in our minds that we must not outwit others but have to convince them. Our posture, accordingly, is not one of deviousness but of frank objectivity. We have not proposed ourselves as mere go-betweens but have tried to be honest brokers. It is a question not of whether we want to give offense in Paris or London but of putting through what is possible. As to how far our ability will reach, time will have to tell.

The entry applications of Great Britain, Ireland, Denmark, and Norway, as well as the Swedish note of the early summer of 1967, afforded one of the grand options in European politics. They posed certain questions: Should and must the abyss between the Western European countries go on existing? Should and must European states with a democratic tradition and economic maturity be excluded from the work of unification? In both cases the answer was bound to be only no. On the German side we carefully scrutinized all the related problems, and we concluded that these problems would be solved through that same good will without which the establishment in its time of the EEC would have been impossible.

The procedure for the entry applications was initiated by requesting the European Commission to report to the Council of Ministers. By the end of September 1967 it presented a comprehensive picture of the problems that would crop up during the negotiations with respect to entry. From the very outset we endorsed the principle that newly entering states must accept the treaty itself and all the decisions that had already been based on it. They would also have to be prepared to adopt as their own all the general aims of the EEC for the future. Together with the commission we were of the opinion that the economic problems bound up with entry would be soluble if a positive political decision on the part of the member states led first to negotiations. The problems analyzed in the commission's document, including such complicated ones as agrarian and currency questions, should, in our opinion, soon be clarified by conversations with Great Britain and the other countries prepared to enter.

We have made clear our attitude within the community, in consultations and discussions with the interested parties, and in public statements. We have emphasized that this historic opportunity must not be missed. We have not been light-minded about doubts and objections. To be sure, of course, it also had to be asked what situation would arise if the extension of the European community did *not* come about. We said in advance that there was no question here of a simple situation. Nor could it be denied that the economic drifting apart in Western Europe had already created grave problems for a number of countries. Denmark, which is very close to us, was hit particularly hard.

The economic motives that argued and still argue for the inclusion of Great Britain and the other states in the Common Market are obvious: A broader division of labor makes more rational production and a better distribution system possible; intensive competition strengthens the dynamic forces. Because Great Britain alone is a market of 55 million consumers (compared with 180 million in the EEC and 60 million in the Federal Republic) with a gross national product in order of magnitude between that of the Federal Republic and that of France, Great Britain's entry would raise the production and the economic capabilities of the EEC by a third. If the other EFTA countries were to unite with the EEC, the economic potential of the community would increase by more than a half.

Great Britain can demonstrate significant technical achievements in many areas; for instance, in space and air travel, rocket and atom technique, and computers. This know-how within the Common Market would lead to a rapid heightening of productivity, and Europe would be in a better position to maintain itself vis-à-vis the technology of the super-powers. It is just in this domain that Prime Minister Wilson has made some notable suggestions.

The general economic advantages of entry would be counterweighted by transitional difficulties. In individual areas—for instance, coal and textiles—the competition would become more acute. But we were and are convinced that sensible regulations can be found.

In our opinion there would be no excessive encumbrances arising out of Great Britain's political position either. During the period of the dismantling of their position as a world power the British attempted at first to make use of the historically and culturally evolved relations with the United States—their "special relationship"—in such a way that positions that had been lost might be compensated for as far as possible. But the shift of power in favor of the superpowers detracted a great deal from the significance of Great Britain's special relationship to the United States. England found itself embarking, though rather reluctantly, on a course toward a more intimate connection with the Continent. Even before the entry application Harold Wilson declared that Great Britain would as member of the EEC participate to the fullest extent in all political discussions within the community. The identification of British policy with the growing political unity of the Continent would, he said, have two important consequences: The endeavors on behalf of a détente between East and West could be better coordinated, and a Europe that had been increased by Great Britain would be able to play a bigger role in the world. From our point of view this could only be agreed with.

At a press conference in November 1967 President de Gaulle announced that France would not agree to the acceptance of negotiations with respect to entry. Earlier, to be sure, he had not wanted to exclude the possibility of Great Britain's ultimately mooring its ship alongside the Continental quai. Until then there might be, as he said, some "arrangement" possible.

On the German side we did not at all rule out the settling of commercial or other questions prior to negotiations on entry. But this did not in any way alter our conviction that the problems bound up with the entry of Great Britain and the other countries could be solved. We continued to maintain that the desire to bridge over the chasm between the EEC and the EFTA and the idea of an economic union through the extension of the European communities would finally be effectuated.

We never regarded the entry of Great Britain and the other states as an event that could be accomplished in a very brief period of time. We knew that the requisite negotiations would take time, but we thought it a mistake to delay or indeed to block the acceptance of negotiations. It was our view that the extension of the communities could no longer be dismissed from European discussion. We were bound to take as our initial position that the communities themselves would assume their final form only after the solution of this question too. This position did not imply that we wanted to block the further progress of the communities. On December 15, 1967, immediately prior to the interim decision made by the Council of Ministers of the EEC, the Federal parliament appealed to the cabinet to seek to obtain a decision on the opening of negotiations with respect to entry. I expressed my own view in reporting on the state of the negotiations and added:

The commission recommends that negotiations be entered into. This decision must be made on December 19. This view is also shared by my colleagues from Italy and from the Benelux countries. I myself am prepared for a long night on December 19 so that we know where we are and how things are to proceed. We want to end up on December 19 with a clear conclusion to be put on record by its chairman. We shall resolutely advocate the opening of governmental negotiations.

If the first step, in the sense of official governmental negotiations, is not taken now, then all participants will have to examine the situation that will have come about—each government for itself and the governments with one another, all, or some with each other and in relation to others inside and outside the community. In this connection, in addition to Franco-German and Anglo-German conversations, efforts might also be made by The Five, in the interest but not in lieu of the European community.

I also referred to the fundamental rule of the community, that the formation of opinion had to take place on the basis of the opinions of all parties. A few days before, I had met in Chequers with Harold Wilson and George Brown and with the Social Democratic leaders from other countries. This encounter was not particularly useful, but nevertheless I was able to ascertain that in the given situation the British government—wholly justifiably—wanted to know only whether negotiations would be accepted or not. There was no room for considerations that were aimed at interim solutions. What was to be feared in case of a failure to come to an agreement was obvious. On this point I said the following to the Federal parliament:

> The danger that cannot be mistaken lies in this, that the thinking in terms of the community might be harmed, indeed, would with some certainty be harmed, if the impres-

sion were to arise that the one-sided conclusion of a *single* government, if it led to a negative result, could determine the rule of action. It is to be feared that the élan needed to take the great decisions lying before the community might fail. Even now it is unmistakable that other extensions will be affected by blocking the entry of Great Britain. There is a threat of stagnation of what has come into being as the achievement of the European community. We would like the extension without endangering what has already been created. It will be difficult to come to any agreement concerning the transition to the final phase of the community as long as the questions of entry are not clarified. It would be wrong for me not to emphasize the seriousness of the situation expressly and vigorously. The government of this Federal Republic of ours does not have its being in the categories of power claims, demonstrations, and least of all threats. But our own interest, which it is up to us to represent, and our understanding of the state of European interests obliges us to speak a clear language and urge our French neighbors not to make things too difficult for themselves and others.

Before it became clear on December 19 in the Council of Ministers in Brussels that because of the French attitude there was not going to be any unanimity with respect to the acceptance of negotiations on entry, I said the following there:

> There can be no doubt that we are at a portentous stage in the European community and with respect to European cooperation in general. It remains to be ascertained whether and in what form the work of European unification can be extended and perfected.
>
> The German delegation left no doubt that it considered it right to enter into negotiations with Great Britain, Ireland,

Denmark, and Norway and also to deliberate on the letter from the Swedish government. In spite of a number of unmistakable difficulties we shall regard it as a major step forward if during the next few years we are in the position of strengthening our Europe economically and also of allowing it to become more effective than before in the organization of peace.

For more than half a year the applications for entry have been lying on the table. In Item Number 194 of its report of September 29 the commission recommended that negotiations be begun for the further clarification of the questions cast into relief by the applications. Problems related to the applications have been of deep concern to the European governments, the community, and European public opinion. I believe that both the importance of the subject and the dignity of the community, its member states, and the governments making application warrant that a clear answer now be given as to whether negotiations are to be initiated or not. At the same time I should like to emphasize that the Rome treaty does not allow us to shelve the applications for entry without negotiations with those applying. Nor has this been suggested by any party. I have rather gained the impression that the extension of the community has been affirmed *in principle* by all six of the member governments.

In its deliberations during the past few months the German government has taken those points of view that favor extension, as well as the objections that have been made, as seriously as the subject warrants. The repeated discussion in the EEC Council of Ministers, as well as the conversations that the governments have conducted with one another, have permitted the problems that must be solved in the negotiations to emerge clearly. The comprehensive and painstaking report of the commission has proven particularly helpful.

In assessing all the difficult problems—politicoeconomic, commercial, agrarian, currency—that are thrown up by the extension of the community, I should like to say flatly that in our view not one of these problems is insoluble. To be sure, there must be present that degree of resolution for cooperation that ought to characterize the European policy of our times. Like all the other partners within the community, we, too, know that the individual problems that are to be solved touch on significant economic interests of the individual countries. The German delegation has now arrived at the same point as the commission. Any further clarification cannot, in our opinion, be found by way of studies and conversations between The Six but only by initiating negotiations with the applicants. Only in such negotiations will it be possible to ascertain if the states wishing to enter are ready and in a position to take over the rules of the treaty and the regulations that have been passed since then in such a way that the healthy development of the community is vouchsafed and all dangers of any enduring economic disadvantage for all participants avoided. I should like to emphasize that we have reached agreement on the general obligations that every new member state must assume, that is, the acceptance of the treaties and of their political goals, as well as acceptance of the decisions since the acceptance of the treaties.

We are familiar with the problems that will constitute the primary object of the discussions between the community and its member states on the one hand and the applicant states on the other. We are also familiar with the points of view of the six member governments. We are not, however, cognizant of how the British government and the other governments conceive the solution of these questions in detail. In this connection I am thinking, for instance, of the position of the pound sterling and the regulations for a number of Commonwealth countries, as well as of the rhythm and the determination of the requisite transitional periods. On the other hand, the applicant governments will probably be interested to get to know our opinion on important questions. Here I am thinking of the duration and the shaping up of the transitional measures, and the modalities of adaptation provided for in the treaty, as well as the future formation of joint agrarian financing. It is only on the basis of such negotiations that The Six will be able to arrive at a unitary point of view concerning rights and duties, advantages, and performances of the states wishing to enter.

I think there is a common conviction, shared by the British government, that as long as Great Britain's economy is still not really consolidated, the economic development of the community will also suffer diminution. An important prerequisite for such a consolidation is, however, for Great Britain to base its future economic orientation on solid assumptions. Only in negotiations can trustworthy perspectives for Great Britain's further economic policy be established. For this reason, too, the community must offer a clear answer, which cannot be given by way of indefinite promises and optional procedures. A positive acceptance of the application for negotiation ought to entail the effective and enduring revival of the British economy that we all wish for.

For the inner development of the community, too, which we are all striving for, as well as for a continuing and secure economic development in our countries, such a step forward will create the requisite climate of confidence. We cannot permit ourselves, either politically or economically, to let uncertainty concerning the fate of the entry applications prevail within the community for any length of time.

As we know from experience, negotiations require a cer-

tain lapse of time. Our British partners have told us that
they wish to enter the community only with a healthy economy; restoring the economy will also take a certain length of
time. Decisive reasons support the view that both—the process of consolidation and the negotiations—should be allowed
to run parallel to each other. If we can make up our minds
now to the acceptance of negotiations, a chronologically
optimum solution could be found for both sides—Great
Britain and the community—quite independent of the psy-
chologically favorable effect that the acceptance of negotiations wil exercise on the process of consolidation, in which
we, too, have an interest. Great Britain's latest currency and
economic measures are an important step forward. Our community, which during the past few years has consolidated
itself economically to such an astounding degree, should
not now for its own part fail in courage and vision.

Understandably, the Foreign Minister of the Federal Republic of Germany would much regret casting a vote on this
important question that was different from that of his
French colleague. We—France and Germany—are close to
each other in other areas of European politics, and we remain
dependent on each other. In this connection, however, I must
also be allowed to refer to Article 5 of the Rome treaty,
which enjoins every member state to desist from any measures
that might jeopardize the realization of the aims of the treaty.
The treaty mentions the enlargement of the community as
one of its goals. The treaty prescribes negotiations to this
end. Every member is free with respect to the final, material
decision. But no one may block the road that according to
the treaty leads to a decision concerning the acceptance of
new members.

The German government regards it as necessary that negotiations, in the sense of Article 237 of the Rome treaty, be

initiated with Great Britain, as well as Ireland, Denmark, and Norway. The application of the Swedish government for conversations concerning a cooperation that is to be as comprehensive as possible should also be decided affirmatively. What is at stake now is whether or not we wish to and can speak out jointly for negotiations on entry. If that is not yet possible, the applicant governments must be informed nevertheless of the interim result.

But even in the event that the delegations do not vote unanimously, I take as my starting point that the entry applications will remain on the agenda of the Council of Ministers. They will remain, in any case, on the agenda of Europe.

This was the vote of the Federal Republic in December 1967. It met with a French rejection, as was to be foreseen. But three concordant statements were made that we regard as important points of linkage: First, it was emphasized that no fundamental objection to the extension of the community was validated. Second, there was a general agreement, especially with respect to Great Britain, that there was a connection between economic stability and entry. The French speaker, to be sure, somewhat expanded this point, for practically speaking he made total consolidation of the British economy a precondition for any negotiations on entry. Third, it was unanimously observed that the question of entry would remain on the agenda of the Council of Ministers. And it was this last decision that is crucial.

7

FOR
A GREATER
EUROPE

The theme of the extension of the EEC remains on the agenda of European policy making. The British government did not withdraw its entry application; nor did the other countries. Nevertheless, there was nothing surprising about the fact that the Brussels interim response was widely interpreted as a veto and was commented on in correspondingly bitter terms. It could only be hoped that the proverbial British composure would prove itself in this situation, too.

I was surely not the only one who remembered the role that Great Britain had played on behalf of the freedom of Europe. On January 18, 1968, at a dinner in honor of the leading representatives of the Luxemburg resistance I said:

> When Europe was lying in ruins after this tragic war, it was Winston Churchill, in his great speech in Zurich in 1946, who demanded European unity and appealed for a reconciliation between Germany and France.
>
> Much of this has become reality since. It was not in vain that, in addition to Robert Schuman, de Gasperi, and Adenauer, Spaak, Luns and Bech, two Englishmen were awarded the Charles Prize in Aix-la-Chapelle.

And now Great Britain is knocking on the gate of the European Economic Community. As a European I ask myself, somewhat bewildered, why Great Britain must knock. Did it not prove, in Europe's darkest hours, that it belonged to it? I was in Scandinavia at that time, others were in London, still others were listening in to London—but at that time we all knew that Great Britain stood for and suffered for and was consuming itself for freedom. Gratitude may not be a political category, but forgetfulness can scarcely agree with us either.

The transition from its historical attitude toward the world to a new role in Europe is not, of course, so easy for the British as some think. Even in authoritative British circles it was possible very recently to encounter quite divergent conceptions of the character of the Common Market and of the political possibilities of the EEC. Needless vexations were caused by an occasional announcement coming from London of some overemphatic claim to leadership. But in a growing Europe it is not a question of who is leading the parade: it is a question of dismantling old conceptions of hegemony, not of cultivating new ones. We ourselves have disaccustomed ourselves to claims of leadership and do not wish to be confronted by a choice between French and British leadership. In the European community we are, despite all difficulties, about to develop new forms of joint decision making. I should not like to be a party to any old-fashioned triangular relationships between Paris, London, and Bonn. Aside from anything else, this would constitute a disregard of our other neighbors.

In spite of the indicated difficulties of the British in adapting themselves to the new European facts and necessities, there has never been any doubt that Great Britain, once the

prerequisites are laid down, will be a loyal member of the
community and especially observant of the treaty. Its experience will prove of value to the libertarian content and the
democratic structure of the community.

For some time now this has been, independently of the
theme of entry, an area full of cares. It would be premature
to pursue here the far-ranging ideas dealing with a European
parliament based on direct elections, but the terms of reference of the European parliament formed of delegates from
national representative bodies are too narrow. The elaboration of the EEC will withdraw more and more substantive decisions from the sphere of the national parliaments
without an appropriate shifting of parliamentary controls
and cooperation onto the European level. This will only be
remedied by extending the spheres of competence of the
European parliament.

The Scandinavian countries, too, would contribute forces
of freedom to the European union. Our continental thinking
has made us far too inclined to underestimate the importance of the countries of the European north, but Europe
derives its strength from the diversity of its nations and
states. Europe would make itself needlessly poorer if the
Scandinavian countries were to remain on the outside; in
their flourishing culture and in their economic capabilities
they are able to do much that is exemplary. Its countries
have a strong tradition of international cooperation, have
been involved in projects of peace and humanity, and have
spiritual and material reserves of significance for the development of European cooperation. I therefore say that
Europe requires the creative energies of its Scandinavian
members; the north has an important task in Europe.

At this time it is still impossible to foresee how the questions that have arisen as a result of the deferred entry appli-

cations will be dealt with. To be sure, there seemed to be clear signs during the first few months of 1968 that all parties were concerned with not allowing what had been achieved in the EEC to be endangered, still less destroyed. At the same time, it is true, our warning that a lack of unity concerning the questions of entry would make more difficult any progress within the EEC was confirmed.

On the German side we have been obliged to put up with the fact that our policy of accommodation has not been understood and approved by everyone. If one is carrying on an independent policy, one must not be afraid of the reproach of falling between two stools; we sat down not between two stools but on our own stool. It was not that we lacked resolution but that we were guided by the endeavor to avoid any unnecessary harm to European cooperation while at the same time coming closer to the goal recognized to be the correct one.

We have therefore concentrated our efforts on measures and agreements that do not replace the entry of Great Britain but prepare the way for it as effectively as possible. This endeavor has entailed considerations, including those of an institutional nature, as to how the gulf between the EEC and the states wishing to enter it might be bridged over. Further, we have attempted to clear up the question of whether a commercial-political "arrangement" could be contrived that would have a genuine effect from the point of view of entry, that is, in the sense of a gradual growing together of the national economies so that not only would duties arise but also rights would be established. We also raised the question whether adherence to Euratom should be settled first, because the economic and political problems related to the enlargement of the EEC do not apply to Euratom.

The British government has remained very skeptical of

all references to "interim solutions" or "phasing plans." It has seemed to count more on those suggestions made by the Benelux foreign ministers that—with France or without—envisage cooperation in areas that are not taken in by the community treaties. Nor have we excluded the study of such possibilities. When Federal Chancellor Kiesinger and I were in Rome at the beginning of February 1968 we found ourselves in agreement with Italian statesmen—President Saragat, Premier Moro, Vice-Premier Nenni, Foreign Minister Fanfani—that serious efforts must be undertaken to avoid a setback for the segment of public opinion in Great Britain that is sympathetic to the idea of Europe. When we were in Paris in the middle of February, we were obliged to perceive that it was not going to be easy to develop a unanimously supported policy of a step-by-step rapprochement.

But on February 16, 1968, both governments established as a joint conviction their wish for the extension of the communities. Also, an "arrangement" was outlined—in the perspective of the entry of Great Britain and the others—including a progressive reduction of customs for industrial goods and agreements for agricultural products. We were also in agreement about the wisdom of extending technological cooperation beyond the circle of The Six. The British government had already devoted particular attention to this category of problems in the preceding months.

In the given circumstances no substantive progress can be expected, at least in the short run, to bring about a meeting of minds on political cooperation. I find it also difficult to imagine that additional political consultations could change anything now. There has never been any shortage of opportunities for exchanges of opinion in Western European and Atlantic institutions. It is quite another matter that one must clear up in one's own mind the problems that will confront the European community—independent of the relationship to Eastern Europe—both economically and potically during the coming years.

Here it is a question, after all, not only of the extension of the EEC through the entry, sooner or later, of Great Britain, Ireland, and the Scandinavian states but of an appropriate association between the community and our neighbors immediately to the south, that is, Austria and Switzerland, in keeping with their neutral status. Our special economic and neighborly interest in this extension is understandable and should not be assessed by the Soviet Union with any hostility. If in the north, Sweden finds its place in an extended community, an objective settlement for Finland will be facilitated. Like Austria, or even more so, Finland is dependent on good relations with the Soviet Union but at the same time must be concerned with preventing any harm to its export interests in the markets of the West.

Also at issue is what might be called the future Mediterranean policy of the community. In the East there are the associational treaties with Greece and Turkey, but in the West suitable forms will have to be developed for economic cooperation with Spain and Portugal. Other questions arise out of the treaties with the North African states, Israel, and Yugoslavia.

I have mentioned Greece. I must add the oppressive effect on many of us in Germany of the political crisis in this friendly country. On October 13, 1967, I said to the Federal parliament that it would not be hypocritical or imply any meddling in the affairs of another state to say:

> The events in Greece, the abolition of basic rights, and the turning aside from democracy have given us great concern. In the Committee of Ministers of the Council of

Europe the Federal government will join in deciding on the results of the inquiries and the recommendation of the committee pursuant to the complaint under Article 24 of the European Convention for the Protection of Human Rights. Our sole concern in this will be humanity, legality, and democracy, and also the kindred question of the reliability of organizations we are part of.

We do not feel ourselves to be political moralists. I know, moreover, that the interests of one's own country cannot be adequately represented by means of an ideologically constricted foreign policy. However, the destruction of parliamentary democracy, the cancellation of human rights, the fate of political prisoners cannot leave us indifferent, especially when this touches the European community indirectly or indeed directly. In Germany, to be sure, we know from our own experience how little one people can be helped from outside in finding its own way anew to a democratic state based on laws or, for that matter, in constituting it for the first time.

No one should be surprised if we say that dictatorships do not suit the European community; they lead to encumbrances for Western cooperation. And no one should presume anything but this: the sympathies of European democrats are for freedom and justice and for those who must suffer on behalf of freedom and justice. But we must also grasp the complexities of a contemporary situation—which we cannot discuss at this point—and not neglect our own interests or make any improvement of relations more difficult.

8

THE
COURAGE
TO SAY YES—THE
WEAKNESS OF SAYING NO

Our policy on Europe must not stand against something; it must stand for something. And it must link itself vigorously to the requirements of the scientific and technical revolutions.

The beginnings of the policy of European unification after 1945 were in point of time and in their political logic partially—yet surely not only—parallel to the growing threat from the East. The initial unification in the West was conceived by many as a consequence of the Cold War. Some people thought that integration was the political rounding off of what had been the military assignment of NATO, with the sole aim of setting up a dam against communism. In this way the policy on Europe was given a defensive, all-too-narrow or even negative content.

The Cold War of the postwar years lies behind us but difficult confrontations continue that cannot be overcome by illusions, or by becoming prisoners of outmoded formulations of questions. I consider the policy on Europe to be stronger if it is not explained by mere anticommunism.

Rather, Europe should be unified for the good of the European peoples and for their constructive role in the world, and the policy of European statesmen must be harmonized with the long-range goal of a European peace order.

Not only the West but also the East is becoming aware of the importance of all-European cooperation. Slowly, and it is to be hoped not too late, it will become clear that the cooperation and unification of Europe is not directed against anyone. In a dangerous epoch and in a strife-divided world it could, rather, be an example of how nations and states, regardless of different kinds of governmental and social systems, can achieve prosperity and security by peacefully working together.

Reconciliation and cooperation, which we are striving for between West and East, have already become a fact in Western Europe and will succeed in spite of the above-described difficulties. The economic and political unification of Europe is a substantive element of a worldwide peace.

It is true that Europe can no longer consider itself the center of spiritual and economic progress in the world. In disunion our continent would only sink still further, but in cooperation it will have a great deal to offer mankind. If that is what we want, we not only must overcome political obstacles, but also must be prepared to participate in the explosive scientific and technical developments that, in the future, will determine the face of the world.

Europe must not slide into a peripheral position in relationship to the world powers. Steam engines could be built by individuals; airplanes were much more difficult; in space travel, orders of magnitude have been attained that transcend the powers of individual European states. Thus, in our modern world, politics can no longer be thought of as independent of the effects of technological progress. These effects to a great extent will determine the future international significance of states and their coexistence. The scientific-technical, the economic, and the political potential of the individual states is governed today by direct interdependence. The viability of states in the future will depend more and more strongly on their participation in and their contribution to technological progress. The necessity of living up to the effects of technological development touches all the key areas of foreign policy. This factor is as relevant to our efforts on behalf of a peaceful and satisfactory future for Europe as it is to the relationships between industrial countries and underdeveloped countries.

Although the population of the earth is now growing by 70 million people a year, 25 million people starve to death every year. The developed countries in the West and East, in spite of their well-known conflict, are confronted by the question of whether or not they are capable of making a joint effort against hunger and poverty; only if such a joint effort is successful, presumably will they be able to avoid explosive developments in the relationship between North and South.

The population explosion and the scientific revolution are the two great moving forces of our time. The major developments in the future will no longer be derived only from power-political or ideological constellations but also to a large measure from economic and technological capabilities. If the atomic war of destruction is avoided, which every reasonable person must wish for with every fiber of his being, and if it is true that peaceful nuclear science, space travel, cybernetics, and modern biology transgress all ideologies and lead up to a community of thinking, then the political difficulties of our backward present will become transitional difficulties—difficulties that will be soluable.

An economic community during the coming decade is

thinkable only if it is at the same time a closely knit community of scientific and technological progress, a community
for the coordinated, peaceful exertion of strength. When we
learn to think in categories like these it will be easier to
link together enduringly the West of our continent with its
East. This progress, which is the only thing that can ensure
our common future, must now be reflected on and initiated.
For this the preconditions must be created within the individual states.

It is precisely ourselves, in the Federal Republic of Germany, who must not succumb to any soothing dreams of the
future. It is precisely ourselves who must be clear in our
minds that a phase has been introduced into the history of
mankind in which the importance, the weight, and the influence of a state will depend on whether or not it is capable of
mobilizing the capital of its talents. We shall have to realize
that we still have a research deficit and also an underdeveloped interaction between scientific and political practice.
In former years our means and capabilities were linked up
far too much, to the detriment of our research, with short-
range defensive thinking. I consider that we must now
demonstrate an ambition for scientific and technical expansion, that our society must be put in the position of radically
modernizing itself.

It is old-fashioned to think that we are giving ourselves
the luxury of too much expensive educational training. It is
more accurate to say that we cannot afford to let even one
person fail to take advantage of a vocational or college
education if he is capable of it. It is a question here of the
potential inherent in many families of the broad strata of
our people. The percentage of workers' children among
students, in comparison with Western industrial states, is
still frighteningly low. We have an untapped reservoir that

is to be explained by the peculiarities of a slowly changing and excessively heterogeneous school system in different parts of our Federal Republic. Finally, there is also a female reservoir that must be tapped if a mockery is not to be made of all the talk about modernity and equality of rights.

It is also the point of European unification that our continent must be able to link itself swiftly and purposefully to the dimensions of the twenty-first century. If the European communities extend and develop themselves, Europe's role in the world, economically and politically, will be greater. European unification is meant, after all, to serve that consistent policy of peace by means of which the political tensions between East and West can be overcome. We are convinced that the cooperation that the Western European countries have already found themselves ready for will also be of decisive importance for the relations between Eastern and Western Europe. Western European unification not only is no obstacle for the accommodation of interests but will prove itself to be a factor that promotes and stabilizes that accommodation.

The Soviet Union and the other Eastern European countries are well advised to view the European communities realistically. The economic capabilities of an expanding European Economic Community will make commerce between East and West even more profitable and attractive. Here I am thinking of an intensified exchange of technological knowledge, an area for cooperation between East and West that is of vital consequence for the peace and welfare of the European nations.

For us there is no contradiction between the unification of the Western European countries and cooperation with Eastern Europe. The Western countries, magnified by unification, should encourage the dialogue with Eastern Europe,

D

beginning a collaboration based on mutual interests over and beyond the differences of systems. The cooperation and the unification of Europe correspond to the logic of our times, one that in the long run can elude no one. It is only through the fusion of the limited forces of the individual nations that we can create a fitting importance for the voice of Europe. Only in this way shall we Europeans be self-conscious and strong enough to assume a full responsibility for the preservation of world peace and the welfare of nations.

European relations with the United States have proved themselves viable in the domain of commercial policy in the Kennedy Round; such cooperation will be extended to other domains as well. The vision of an independent Europe that will speak with a *single* voice and will stand beside the United States as an equal can then become a reality. Even now the cooperation between the two, although not very spectacular, is effective. We are struggling to intensify that cooperation. And I think that in this age of scientific-technical revolution we Europeans no longer must remain preponderantly those who take; here, too, we can arrive at a harmonious partnership.

9

AMERICA
A PARTNER

Friendship with the United States—by now a matter of course—is an important element of our foreign policy, as is the alliance that the United States and we belong to.

Because its decisions affect the fate of the entire world, our relations with the United States are different and more complex than our relations with states that are farther away from this position of power and responsibility. Our relations with the United States are not merely based on the calculation of interests.

If the Federal Republic is following a line of greater independence in its foreign policy today, no estrangement from America can be deduced from this. No German statesman aware of his responsibilities—and for that matter no German at all in the Federal Republic whose memory is still intact—would wish or be able to forget that our ascension to economical prosperity and our evolution in Western Europe is due in special measure to the postwar policy of our American partner. How could a former Mayor of Berlin forget that! Did he not witness his city being saved from Stalin and its citizens from starvation?

When Germany—and together with it a large portion of Europe, because of German culpability—was lying in ruins and political reform was hampered by drab material need, the United States voluntarily assumed a responsibility that has been more than a matter of course. It was the United States that, through the open-handed help given by the Marshall Plan, made it possible for our part of Europe to gather together the requisite strength for its reconstruction, and at the same time it provided a military shield for that helpless Europe.

The result of this situation was the North Atlantic Treaty Organization, in which the responsibility borne by America found an equivalent in the united responsibilities of the European partners. It was no small matter for Germany, the instigator and loser of World War II, to be accepted in this alliance as a fully equal member. This must be admitted even by those who in the early 1950s might have wished for a more flexible Western policy and who were harassed by the doubt as to whether all possibilities in foreign policy had really been put to the test.

In any case we Germans have found a first-rate ally in the United States not only for Western security but also as a reliable representative of our own vital interests, as is quite visible to everyone even today in West Berlin.

In the Federal government statement of December 13, 1966, it was said that in relation to the United States we had during the preceding years sometimes overemphasized our own cares and needs and overlooked the fact that even a great power like the United States has its cares and problems—problems for which it expected some understanding and support from its allies.

Almost against its will, since the last war this powerful nation has gotten itself into commitments on all continents. We shall not forget this, and we should consider—as the government statement was worded—how we for our part and how Europeans as a whole might be able to assume joint responsibility for the preservation of world peace and for the welfare of all nations more decisively than before.

The American commitment in Europe cannot be depreciated by maintaining that the United States was only serving its own security: the consolidation of a strategic outpost, industrial expansion, and the conquest of markets for the sale of its goods. Views like these, which are occasionally heard from the extreme right and the extreme left, merely challenge positive contradiction. Nevertheless, there is a problem of "Americanization" in the economic and technological domain, as many Americans are also aware. The American President's admonitions and the measures he has taken for safeguarding the dollar are an impressive indication of America's intentions. We must realize clearly that the problems involved cannot be solved by emotions but only by work and by a partnership based on mutual confidence.

The partnership between America and Europe is not a grocers' union but is based on ideas of freedom that have been fought for and realized in different ways and with varying success in both continents. Western Europe has become stronger and more self-aware under the shield of America. Its economy already partially integrated, it is having a powerful effect throughout the world and is in competition with all the great industrial nations. Europe is becoming aware of its own strength and of the tasks that will fall to it.

Under such conditions it is only natural for the European states to reconsider their relationship to the premier power of the West. To be sure, the first basic question to be asked is: Can Europe dispense with the protection and the partnership of America?

The commitment of the United States is indispensable for the creation of a solid European peace order. The United States guarantee is of decisive importance for the security of the Federal Republic of Germany. The common desire to maintain the peace in Europe and to make it more secure remains an excellent foundation for the deepening of our friendly and intimate relations.

Franco-German cooperation does not conflict in any way with our relationship to the United States but has a quality of its own. We wish to build our European house together with our neighbors and to settle ourselves in it livably. Most of us know how crucial the role of the United States is in ensuring that this house not be destroyed by tempests.

The American presence in Europe is not a goal in and for itself. It serves our joint security. To be sure, the further development of the military and communications techniques, the accords between East and West, and the successes of the policy of détente might make possible a reduction of the troop strength without endangering mutual security. We ought to speak of this sensibly and not allow decisions to be imposed on us either by wishful thinking or by the temporary difficulties of the balance of payments.

At the same time it should never be forgotten that the North Atlantic alliance and the sought-after European-American partnership must go far beyond the realm of military security. The economic and political unification of Europe lies in the interest of the European nations just as much as in that of the United States. Our American friends have told us that Europe must learn to speak with a *single* voice. That means that it will have to be *European* voice.

John F. Kennedy, in his brief period, did a great deal not only to give Western policy a persuasive slant but also to redefine the relationship between Europe and America,

thus developing a clear view of the relations between East
and West. My assessment has not varied since 1964:

   The strategy of peace proclaimed by President Kennedy
is to be assessed as a comprehensive attempt to change the
relationship between East and West without illusions. It is
the attempt to blunt the atomic balance of terror and to
work toward the peaceful solution of problems.
   This strategy is aimed at not allowing the status quo to become congealed, but to transform it step by step and to overcome it.
   At the same time we must make it clear beyond all doubt
that Germany has an interest in détente and not in the maintenance of tension. But for any détente worthy of the name
what is required are just those measures that will help to
overcome the political causes of the tension. And here the
German question cannot be by-passed.
   We learned from Kennedy to stand on the groundwork
of the facts with both feet, but not to become the prisoners
of the moment—to see the world as it is, but to think beyond mere defense; to do everything necessary for freedom,
but to think ourselves into a world of better cooperation. In
the long run a state cannot be stronger externally than it is
internally. This means that creative forces must be awakened
within. They have a value all their own. And for our relations abroad they are not to be eschewed.
   I stand behind the strategy of peace that John F. Kennedy
developed and that President Johnson has vigorously continued.
   The conception developed by Kennedy on June 26, 1963,
at the Free University of Berlin is still embodied in the policy
of the United States. This means that the struggle for piece-
meal changes for the better remains the policy of the lead-

ing Western power. For some time now I have come to the conclusion that that is the only way possible. With the formula of "all or nothing" it may be possible to satisfy emotional impulses but not to carry on a sensible foreign policy.

I did not wait to become Foreign Minister to point out—in Germany and in America—that there is really no need for anyone to be concerned if Europe shows a growing independence and self-awareness, but only if we allow no doubt to remain about the impossibility of any security for Europe in the foreseeable future without the military commitment of the United States. We must say just as distinctly that America could not itself feel secure without the firmness of its friends in Europe. A strong Europe is the precondition for a partnership on a footing of equality on both sides of the Atlantic.

Achieving such equality is not made impossible by America's atomic superiority, which Europe cannot catch up with. Europeans, however, must have their say in the realm of deterrence and securing peace, as well as in strategic planning and decisions. I said as a German active in politics, and I repeat, that I do not wish my country to dispose of nuclear weapons. The majority of my people feel the same; we do not need such weapons. But Europe must never be defenseless. In one way or another the risk involved in attacking Europe must remain sufficiently great.

The alliance with the United States and the other partners of the North Atlantic pact is vitally important for the future we are capable of foreseeing. It is a fundamental element of our foreign policy.

Though this book deals with European politics and a European peace order, honesty—as well as respect for our American ally—demands that Vietnam not be ignored.

Let me express for myself, first and foremost, a profound compassion for the suffering Vietnamese people. What they have had to endure, in both parts of the country, is a Thirty Years' War transferred into this century. This implies a humanitarian duty. It also implies the urgent desire for a peaceful settlement of the conflict and the willingness to contribute to such a settlement leading up to political consolidation.

The present administration of the Federal Republic has not considered it appropriate to undertake an undischargeable commitment or put itself into an ambiguous light by means of statements of "moral support." Nor has it considered it appropriate to impart public suggestions to the Americans.

In the Federal Republic the escalation of the war has given increasing rise to doubts and concern. It is no surprise that such doubts, particularly with respect to the bombings in the north, were uttered in my own party. In a press report—largely distorted—it was indicated, after a meeting of the Board at the beginning of January 1968, that sympathy had been declared for the suggestions of UN Secretary General U Thant and that reference had been made to the resolutions of the Socialist International. But it was also stated that a readiness for peace on *both* sides was needed in order to arrive at a sensible outcome.

In Vietnam—as I said as chairman of my party in October 1967 in Zurich—we have witnessed an increase in the volume of combat equipment, and at the same time in the United States a monumental debate whether this escalation could bring about a military decision. In North Vietnam, on the other hand, there has been an increased determination to hold out and not give in on any of the points listed as preconditions for the acceptance of peace negotiations. In observing a situation in which obviously no one can win or

D*

be beaten in a traditional way, the world has been a witness to the agony of a people making immense sacrifices, regardless of whether it is living in the north or in the south.

In 1965, during a brief trip to America, I realized clearly that in the Federal Republic we had a completely inadequate conception of what the war in Vietnam meant for the United States, materially and spiritually. It had unleashed a public discussion whose depth and passion are unparalleled during the last twenty years. This war is a milestone in the awareness of the American people of the burdens, responsibilities, capacities, and limits of a world power. It cannot help but influence the future international sense of direction of the strongest Western power.

These interconnections and developments cannot remain a matter of indifference to us. Previous Federal administrations had been unable to explain the scope of these problems to the population. What is incontestable was the determination of the United States to live up to its word and to the consequences of its word. It was also clear that President Johnson in all his decisions had the quite solid support of his own people. This is not contradicted by the fact that his administration evidenced a powerful desire to reach peace in Vietnam and to help in working out positive programs of development in Southeast Asia. Behind this attempt lay the grandiose task of making the peace of the world more secure; there was no turning away of America from Europe and no weakening of its interest in our own part of the world. Although the Vietnam debate in the United States was far more bitter than comparable discussions in Europe, many Americans felt such debate to be a sign of strength. The American discussion showed that openness can make a nation conscious of what in the long run strengthens rather than weakens it.

In February 1966 I went to New York as one of the recipients of the Freedom Award. I wrote as follows to a man who—in an idealistic way—had been offended by this, Norman Thomas, the veteran American socialist:

My friends in America represent very various attitudes concerning the appropriateness, sense, boundaries, and responsibility of the present Vietnam policy of the United States. We Germans are no schoolmasters in world politics. But we should surely not be mere followers either, no satellite that considers everything good and fine that the leading Western power considers correct.

I oppose most particularly any simplifying, objectively unfounded comparisons between Vietnam and Berlin.

Precisely someone like myself, who hopes for a full-bodied détente between East and West, cannot lose sight of the fact that in Vietnam a decision is also being reached as to whether the thesis of the American paper tiger and of the possibility of restricted, surrogate wars against an atomic power, helpless against them, will gain the upper hand. It may be that it is only now that the people of the United States will become fully conscious of and frightened by what a burden it is to be a world power, and how often, unfortunately, the decision for a lesser evil is bound up with it. My impression that President Johnson is striving toward a peace under acceptable conditions has not changed. I am advising my friends in Germany to avoid superficial and extremist utterances.

The war in Vietnam has now been escalated for two years. It has become more cruel, tough and embittered. During that time one argument which two years earlier played an essential part, has lost its significance—the credibility and reliability of the United States. If the United States were to

renounce a military solution, this would not affect the trustworthiness of the United States guarantee vital to the security of Europe, the Federal Republic, and Berlin. The unde-
clared war in South East Asia hampers a further relaxation
of tension between East and West. It implies the risk of
widening. That is why peace in Vietnam is also of direct
interest to Europe and Germany.

The tragedy of a small people that for more than two
decades has not seen peace and is seriously in danger of
being decimated cannot be a matter of indifference to anyone. We cannot look on with indifference as a whole people
grinds itself to pieces on behalf of a cause that could have
been won by peaceful means and still must be. For reasons
of humanity this tragedy cannot put up with disinterested
spectators—it summons to the stage the party of mankind.
Those who would like to consecrate the idea of a total
national war are on the wrong warpath. The goal of a total
victory of one side or the other, a victory that has as a precondition military annihilation, is in reality the renunciation
of any peace that is worthy of the name.

10

A
CHANGING
ALLIANCE

We wish for the consolidation and the further development of the Atlantic alliance in tune with the times. What this calls for is the adaptation of the alliance to the changes in world politics.

For some years Europe has not been shaken by great international crises. In our hemisphere politics is no longer solely, or even primarily, determined by the confrontation of two military blocs. The frozen political fronts are beginning to break up. A gradual reduction of the military confrontation now appears conceivable.

This development would not have come about if the Western allies had not stood together in the great crises of the most recent past and been jointly prepared to repulse all attacks. But has NATO become outdated now that the threat has subsided? Has it made itself superfluous? I do not think so. It will have performed its military task only when its political task has been completed. What is at issue now is to secure what has been achieved and to arrive at an enduring just peace order in Europe.

We are in the decisive years between two eras in which the course is being laid down for a long time to come. Such a thing happens only rarely at spectacular conferences or in momentous political decisions of principle. It is not always wars, crises, and revolutionary movements that determine the course of history. One is reminded of the saying about the ideas that come on the feet of doves and nevertheless lead the world. This saying may apply to the development of Europe during the last few years, for it came about almost unnoticed.

We cannot speak of cooperation in Western Europe or of securing the peace for all Europe without including the North Atlantic alliance in our considerations. Because of the necessary and desired participation of the United States and of Canada the alliance stretches out beyond Europe, yet its center of gravity and its principal mission lie in Europe. This defense alliance is and remains necessary even though a changing world constantly obliges us to reconsider its goals and its methods and to adapt it to developments. Essentially there is nothing new in this. It applies to all unions.

It is well known that a number of members of the alliance would like to improve and strengthen the organs for political consultation and coordination within NATO. This is to be welcomed. We have often made the point ourselves that the East-West policy has as a precondition a certain measure of canvassing of opinion and of communication between the Western partners. This approach remains correct and is worth striving for.

On the other hand, the idea of a "joint policy" within NATO has been turned down, primarily by the French government. It is true that this idea does not involve a joint policy in the literal sense, but there is a divergence of opinion even about the necessity and appropriateness of up-to-date forms of consultation and cooperation. In such circumstances any insistence on far-reaching claims can scarcely be successful. At the same time, however, all the allies seem to be in agreement that the goal of our policy must be an enduring and just peace order throughout Europe, by which I mean an order that will eliminate the causes of tension and overcome the division of Europe.

Moving from an alliance that was concluded in a period of intense international tensions and for the purposes of defense against a very specific danger to a policy of détente very naturally raises a number of new questions that must be answered. A reduction of the tensions between East and West is useful and desirable, yet our policy aims at something further. It regards as its task the elimination of the causes of tension during a phase of the détente and the creation of a situation that as far as human provision can reach will offer no grounds for new and dangerous tensions. The period of détente, which we hope will be enduring, is to be used in order to give European security a solid foundation and to bring about an enduring peace order.

The revolutionary objectives of Soviet policy in Europe have receded; nevertheless the influence of ideology on the Communist leaderships in future must not be underestimated, for it will often distort their analysis of the policies of non-Communist states and societies. More than one conference and publication have even in the most recent period sketched a completely warped image of the West and of its political intentions. Such ideological prejudices restrict the readiness for a detente and for cooperation. They are deeply embedded, and it will not be easy to overcome them.

We have built up our state successfully in the hope that a new, free, and united Europe would be created, in the hope of a European community in which our nation, with equal rights and finally, also, united again, would be able to live side by side with the other nations of our hemisphere. It was toward such a Europe that the Germans in the Federal Republic have directed their policy; it is what they are working for. Our participation in Atlantic cooperation has always been related to our European objectives.

The very constitution of the Federal Republic of Germany permits the transfer of sovereign rights to supranational organizations. The Federal Republic has subordinated all its combat forces to the Supreme Command of NATO. With respect to its allies it has renounced the production of atomic, biological, and chemical weapons, subjected itself to restrictions on the production of other weapons, and accepted controls. In order to avoid any misunderstanding, it was unambiguously laid down in the Federal government statement of December 13, 1966, that we do not aspire to national control over nor national ownership of nuclear weapons.

In short, we have sought a firm anchoring of the Federal Republic of Germany in the Western alliance. We have closely linked our destinies to the alliance and to the Western European union that is being formed under its protection. This affiliation was all the easier for us because our allies accepted our legitimate national objective: the right of self-determination for our nation and a peace treaty that would enable the Germans to live under the roof of a single state.

The North Atlantic Treaty Organization is first and foremost an effective defense alliance. It prevents potential opponents from being tempted to exert political pressure on any one of the allies through military force. But constant effort is required to maintain this defensive strength in the face of constantly advancing technical development. We realize that the commitment in Europe is a great burden on the United States and that some of its citizens feel it is too heavy. It is understandable to ask why a reduction of the burden should not be possible. It will become possible only when the East-West situation permits it. But I am afraid that the time for any significant lightening of the United States burdens has not yet come.

The Atlantic alliance, for the reasons already pointed out, is not summed up by a military assignment. NATO was supposed to be simultaneously an instrument of political cooperation and of an understanding between governments that shared the same fundamental convictions. This goal does not prevent different governments from having different views of different problems, for tensions are characteristic of an alliance of free states during changing international constellations. What is at issue is a constant and at times painful process of adaptation.

The Federal Republic, I said as early as December 1966 before the Council of NATO in Paris, will not evade discussions, based on mutual confidence, of a reform of NATO during the coming years. It wishes to contribute toward a policy of détente between the states of the Warsaw pact and those of the North Atlantic pact, while opposing any danger to the security of any country. The Federal Republic of Germany is no obstacle to the peaceful, secure future that is to the interest of us all. Nor in this respect shall we let ourselves be led astray by the aggressive speeches made against us by Communist leaders in their own countries, in neutral states, and in the countries of our allies.

The North Atlantic pact and its organization may be imperfect; it may not suffice for many of the demands we should be bound to make on any alliance. But that should not seduce us into seeking false alternatives or alternatives that suit ourselves alone, for it must, rather, be a reason for us to improve the alliance in such a way that it can fulfill all the tasks of our own time and of the future.

Bilateral steps are useful for gradually leading East and West together in Europe. Bilateral steps are bound, however, to remain a patchwork and can even lead to great upheavals if they are not linked to the prospect of a European solution. An enduring detente will not prosper against the background of a process of decay in the Western camp. Moreover, any accord at the expense of an ally would be not only short-sighted but dangerous as well.

I know that very little would be solved by a mere call for a return to the unity of a defensive alliance. I am sure that a joint political sense of direction is needed, for a policy of détente requires concrete objectives for negotiation that point beyond the confrontation of military alliances.

It goes without saying that the relationship of the NATO states to the Soviet Union and its allies will never be uniform, nor would that even be desirable. At the Luxemburg NATO conference (June 1967) and on other occasions I have made the point that our policy vis-à-vis the East should be agreed on but must remain elastic. What will be decisive for its success is for each NATO member to keep the alliance in his mind, to defend his allies, and to make their political path easier. The decisions of the members of the Warsaw pact have shown that their initiators hope to split NATO and thus bring about its demise. This hope obviously must be removed before they can begin sympathizing with a policy of détente in more than a merely tactical way.

NATO and a policy of détente are not mutually exclusive. On the contrary, the existence of NATO—that is, its political weight and its readiness to defend our territory against

all attacks—has shown that a policy of tensions and crises
is of no avail. The weakening of NATO would reduce the
possibility of a détente and lessen its effectiveness. The military deterrent has ensured the peace in Europe. It would be
light-minded to encroach upon it and to risk losing what has
been achieved.

There are various indications that the Soviet leadership
and some of its allies have their gaze riveted on the year
1969 in the hope that the alliance will fall to pieces and
that the East might influence this process for its own purposes. Anyone who cherishes this hope must be made to
see that he is pursuing a will-o'-the-wisp. The alliance has
been concluded for an unlimited duration, and I am assum-
ing that it—together with France—will go on existing and
that even a change in the Warsaw pact would under no
circumstances impel the Western allies to give up their
alliance. As long as there is no enduring, just peace order in
Europe, it is not decisive whether the Warsaw pact organization remains in existence or is replaced by some system of
bilateral mutual aid pacts. In other words, a peace order in
Europe will also not eliminate the problem of bilateral pacts.

Our policy of detente is not to be understood in the sense
of underestimating and neglecting the vital importance of
the Western alliance. On the contrary, we have warned
against allowing the bilateral attitude in East-West relations
to grow out of hand. In place of that we have worked
toward having the alliance as a whole take up a stand with
respect to new tasks.

In 1967 NATO, at the instigation of Belgian Foreign
Minister Harmel, took up the future tasks of the alliance
and the procedural methods of fulfilling them, "in order to
strengthen the alliance"—as the Council of Ministers put

it—"as a factor in an enduring peace." These studies were participated in by the NATO partners, including France; we took an active part and made a number of contributions. In spite of all the pessimistic prognoses the broadly based discussion proved that now as before NATO is capable of elaborating fundamental guidelines of policy.

On December 14, 1967, the fifteen foreign ministers put together the result of the studies in the "Report on the Future Tasks of the Alliance." By way of introduction they stated that "the alliance is a dynamic and potent organization that constantly adapts itself to the changing conditions" and by way of conclusion "that the study underlines the importance of the role that the alliance can play during the coming years in the promotion of détente and in the strengthening of peace."

NATO came into being as a defense alliance, in order to preserve peace, freedom, and security in the territory of the allies. This task has remained, but something has been added to it. The comprehensive report makes the following point: "The Atlantic alliance has two principal functions. One is to maintain adequate military strength and political solidarity, in order to deter aggression and other forms of pressure, and to defend the territory of the member countries, in case any aggression should take place." For "As long as the focal questions under dispute in Europe, first and foremost the German question, remain unsolved, the possibility of a crisis cannot be excluded." The second principal function "consists in striving for further progress toward a more stable relationship in which the fundamental questions under dispute can be solved." The allies declare that "it is the foremost objective of the alliance to bring about a just and enduring peace order in Europe in conjunction with appropriate guarantees of security." They have

resolved "to direct their energies toward this goal by means
of realistic measures of détente in the East-West relationship."

Accordingly, we agree with our allies that military security
and a policy of détente do not contradict but supplement
each other. Without the firm support of the alliance we
cannot carry on any policy of détente. Similarly the political
objective of the alliance will not be realized without an East-
West détente.

The foreign ministers did not content themselves with
laying down these guidelines for the future role of the alliance. In order to give expression to the wishes of their governments, they charged the Permanent Council of NATO to
elaborate, on the basis of the unpublished individual results
of the study, proposals for a policy "aiming at a just and
enduring order in Europe, an overcoming of the division of
Germany, and a strengthening of European security. This
will become part of a process of active, constant preparedness
for the time when fruitful bilateral or multilateral discussions of complex questions will become possible between
Eastern and Western nations."

The starting point of the alliance is the conviction that
our future security must rest on two pillars: on the deterrent effect of the alliance, that is, on one-sided precautions
in any given situation; and on realistic measures of mutual
control of armaments, limitation of armaments, and of disarmament. The comprehensive report of the Council of
Ministers asserts by way of logical conclusion: "The allies
are studying measures of disarmament and limitation of
armaments, including the possibility of balanced force reductions. These studies are being intensified. Their active
pursuit reflects the desire of the allies to work for an effective détente with the East."

11

GERMANY AND THE SOVIET UNION: BEGINNING OF A DIALOGUE

In addition to economic and cultural relations between Germany and the Soviet Union we hope for an improvement of the political relationship between the two of us. Because it would not be realistic to expect an abrupt and fundamental change, we are exerting ourselves to attain an understanding step by step.

The special importance of the Soviet Union—it is obvious —is rooted in its position as a world power and for us, to be sure, also in its position as one of the four powers that are still responsible for the problem of Germany. It was no accident that in December 1966 the Soviet Union was mentioned first in the foreign affairs part of the government statement. It is no contradition to acknowledge the Soviet Union as the leading Communist and East European power and at the same time to take cognizance of the differentiations in the Communist world. But we are going a long way in order to be fair to the role of the Soviet Union and not to give it the impression that we are speculating on differences of opinion in the Communist camp.

Thus we have rejected taking any initiative as far as the relations with the People's Republic of China are concerned.

Nor have we pursued the possibility of formalizing our far-from-insignificant trade relations with China.

This does not necessarily mean it might not be in the interest of a peace policy if China collaborated with the family of nations. A possible later settlement of our relations with the People's Republic of China will, however, have to avoid any disturbance of our relationship with friendly Asian governments, primarily Japan, and with the United States, as well as avoid arousing Moscow's suspicion that we might wish to exploit the Soviet's difficulties with China.

The Union of Soviet Socialist Republics has grown to be a world power, but the Soviet world power remains at the same time a European power. In the international situation of rivalry with the United States, of the potential conflict with China, of the incipient unification of Europe, and of the insecurity in other parts of the world that constitutes a challenge to political intervention, the Soviet leadership has shown little or no inclination to give up power positions, even if in doing so it could secure new, better, and safer relationships. This rigidity is what in essence has characterized the Soviet policy in Europe since the first postwar years. European developments have seemed acceptable to the Soviet leadership only insofar as they consolidate its power position. But détente without the reexamination of power positions is a dubious undertaking.

For us Germans the rigid clinging to the status quo is particularly difficult because it does not open up any prospect of overcoming the division of Germany. For Europe as a whole the present state of division cannot be final either. It is difficult to harmonize the rigid Soviet positions with the properly understood interests of Europe, which has a right to its own, peacefully secured existence, as Europeans are becoming increasingly aware. An accommodation of

interests will not be easy, but it must be sought most tenaciously.

There will be no swift transformation of the European
situation. Every sensible foreign policy in this connection
must take into account a time factor. But it would be a grave
mistake for anyone to regard Europe as the petrified excres-
cence of two spheres of power. It is a living community of
peoples and states. And the transformation that some wish
for and others would like to stop is already making itself
manifest.

It is making itself manifest in the West. It is also mani-
festing itself in the East, where the Warsaw pact has long
since ceased to be the conspiratorial community of ideolo-
gists that wrongly advised propagandists still insist on seeing.
This reference is not to be construed as a way of setting up
artificial contradictions between the Soviet Union and the
Eastern European states allied with it. It would be foolish
and short-sighted, and, for that matter futile, for our foreign
policy to speculate on such contradictions; we are not going
to try to play one off against the other. We must accept the
fact that there is a far-reaching identity of interests between
the Soviet Union and its allies in Eastern Europe. But the
uniformity of the Stalin era belongs to the past; ideology has
failed to extinguish national identities. In fact, ideology is
increasingly influenced by national requirements.

In November 1967 the Union of Soviet Socialist Republics celebrated with unmistakable pride the fiftieth anniversary of its revolutionary birth. I said at the time that it
was not our concern to sit in judgment as to whether or not
the great successes that the ruling party won in and for the
country might have been attainable with lesser sacrifices as
well. The chairman of the Social Democratic Party of Germany, who knows some history, also knows that it would be

senseless to try to put history back on the drawing board for revision. Thus I am of the opinion that we had good cause to congratulate the peoples of the Soviet Union and their government for their impressive achievements. Above all we had good cause to condemn once again the agony inflicted on the peoples of the Soviet Union as a result of Hitler's criminal adventurism. We also had good cause to recall those days when Germany and the Soviet Union gave each other mutual help. The Soviet Union of today will have forgotten the one no more than the other.

In this age of transition—and against the background of the division of Germany—it is a difficult enterprise to bring about good relations with the Soviet Union; a great deal of patience is required. We do not wish either our patience or our good will to fail. We owe that to Europe and to our own country. Our democratic Germany must and will oppose the Soviet Union if and for as long as it tries, by pressure or by other methods, to make its own ideas of state and social order an article of export and thus involve itself in other people's internal affairs. But our democratic Germany can be and the German people would like to be a sincere friend of the Soviet Union. To this it might be added that greatness is also capable of showing greatheartedness. It is not that we are begging for this, but a Soviet Union that would respect the vital rights of the German people would not have to be afraid—and not only because it is powerful—of the German people. And we, those Germans of good will—that is, the great majority—want to see to it with equal concern that no danger of war can ever arise again on German territory.

The face of the Soviet Union has been transformed during these past fifty years; the face of Germany, too. What has remained unchanged is the geography that has made the peoples of the Soviet Union and of Germany indirect but close neighbors and keeps them neighbors (always also taking into consideration the vital rights of the Polish people, who want and ought to live within secure frontiers).

A German foreign minister is not in a position to threaten, nor would this be suitable to my disposition. I am merely making a statement, based on experience, when I say that it is not good, it is not wise, to allow a great people in the center of Europe to continue under the tension of its unnatural fragmentation. I am realistic enough to know that the national unity of the German people—the isolated realization of its right to self-determination—is not today on the agenda of practical politics. Only through the unfolding of a historic process will both portions of Germany be brought closer to each other and linked together; and that process revolves around Europe. But one must desire this process, envisage it, and start in. That process is in the German interest, but it is also just as much—I am deeply convinced of this—in the interest of the Soviet Union, in the interest of all our neighbors, to envisage a peace that is secure beyond all need for precautions, beyond any desire for disturbing changes.

The Soviet Union ought to realize that friendship with Germany, as intended by geography, is an important question that will be formulated in a renewed form if not today then tomorrow. For the interest of both peoples demands that a secure peace be created, an accommodation that no one will have to be afraid of.

The situation has become increasingly complex and entails new problems. Nevertheless, we should remember that only a few years ago the situation now prevailing in Europe seemed to many people to be worth striving for. It is, in fact, a great advance over the time of the Cold War and the political freeze. We have gained not much more but a little more freedom of movement. There are many contacts today between the states of Western and of Eastern Europe. Though for a variety of reasons Germany's starting point was more difficult than that of others, the German government is vigorously striving to promote such relations. Meanwhile, we have emphasized again and again that we do not wish to isolate any state—including the other part of Germany.

Our assertion that relations to the Soviet Union occupy a special priority in our considerations corresponds to the realities and to history. We have said to the Soviet Union that we are prepared at any time to initiate a discussion of all the substantive questions in our relations. We are well aware that such a phase of serious talking takes time. We have also declared ourselves ready to deal with the questions that are more swiftly soluble first—for instance; the resumption of negotiations for the conclusion of a trade agreement, the promotion of cultural relations, accords concerning technical and scientific cooperation (including the application of atomic energy to peaceful ends), and the establishment of a direct air connection between Frankfurt and Moscow.

The government of the Soviet Union knows that we are ready to exchange statements banning the use of force. It goes without saying that we do not wish to evade any question whose discussion is of concern to the Soviet Union. Talks have begun in some questions of mutual interest, but it is still impossible to know how far they will lead. At the moment there is no indication that a substantial improvement in relations is in the offing.

I know that the government of the Soviet Union does not wish to speak of German unity for the time being, but I think it does wish to speak about peace in Europe. We too

want that. In details our opinions may still differ considerably, but no one who takes the trouble to have a discussion
with us will be able to maintain that we are militaristic and
revanchist. In reality everyone knows that we include the
German Democratic Republic and the problematic question
of the division of Germany in our offer to renounce force.

The moment the possibility of any discussions—however
difficult—with the Soviet Union looms up, problems will
show themselves in the West, too. The atmosphere, pregnant
with secrecy, that made the word "Rapallo" a symbol and a
nightmare for Western statesmen was and is obviously hard
to eradicate today. In that 1922 treaty we ended the state of
war with Russia. It united an economic cooperation with a
most-favored-nation clause and formulated a mutual renunciation of war indemnities. Many of those who speak
about Rapallo do not know this. Its essence, that is, the
restoration of a normal and—if possible—friendly relationship between Germany and the Soviet Union, remains a task
that cannot be performed by a single-handed feat. It demands tenacity and intense and quiet labor, but also the
readiness of the Soviet Union to investigate together with
us the possibilities of such a course.

I am well aware of the encumbrances of the past. But I
cannot accept attempts made to force the Federal Republic
into a corner where it does not belong. The German people
and the Federal government want peace. I think that the
governmental responsibility of the German Social Democrats offers an additional guarantee. This party has never
agitated for war, and it has never trampled the rights of
man under foot. Of course the Social Democrat Party of
Germany has not always been right. But it has never given
up its political and ethical principles and will never do so
in future, either within the government or outside.

In the spring of 1967 Leonid Brezhnev made the remark, during a visit to East Berlin, that the Federal government had hidden a great stone in its outstretched hand. This was a vivid but false image. We are, happily, well out of the political Stone Age. Nor are there any other treacherous weapons in our hand. The party head of the Soviet Union did not say concretely just how or with what the Federal Republic was threatening its neighbors.

In 1967 the government of the Soviet Union made numerous other allusions to the danger of militarism and neo-Nazism allegedly bound up with German policy. On December 22, the Federal Republic responded to such a Soviet statement of December 8, 1967, saying it took the view that it was no service to the efforts for understanding and détente to initiate a reciprocal polemic:

In June 1967 the Federal government saw fit to suggest to the Soviet government conversations dealing with questions of interest to both sides. To be sure, this also included the support that the Federal government had requested the Soviet government to give it in the prosecution of Nazi criminals.

The German Federal government had hoped that the Soviet government would respond to this initiative by declaring its readiness to engage in constructive talks. Consequently the Federal government deplores the new Soviet government statement, whose threatening tone is unusual in international exchanges.

More particularly, the statement gives a wholly distorted picture of German domestic politics as well as the policy of the Federal government, known throughout the world, of pursuing its aims by exclusively peaceful means. The openly expressed readiness of the Federal government to exchange statements with the Soviet Union and its allies concerning the renunciation of force is a proof of this attitude. The government of the Federal Republic of Germany firmly rejects the statement of the Soviet Union as an interference in its internal affairs and as a distortion of its foreign policy.

The accusations of the Soviet statement are all the more incomprehensible since in the same statement it is accurately maintained that the views and feeling of the majority of the Germans living in the Federal Republic of Germany are by no means to be identified with those of "hard-core revanchists and neo-Nazis." It is this immense majority that is represented by the parties of the German Federal parliament. It is this majority whose will it is that bears aloft the peace policy of the Federal government.

The German people and its constitutional organs will be able to protect the fundamental order of society based on liberty and democracy. The Federal government hopes that the Soviet Union will contribute its share so that the German people can regain its unity by peaceful means and be able to make its own contribution to a European peace order.

The question still remains, to be sure, whether the difficulties that the Soviet Union made for the Federal government surprised us or whether we had foreseen them. I have never for a moment believed in any rapid improvement of our relationship with Moscow. It is true that I also did not expect the government of the Soviet Union to identify itself, to the extent to which this has happened, with the hostile attitude of East Berlin toward the government of the Great Coalition. In December 1966, for instance, there was still no indication that Moscow would set up as many obstacles to the establishment of diplomatic relations with the Eastern European states as proved to be the case. There is some reason to think that the exaggerated polemic had to serve

as an instrument for holding the Warsaw pact together—
and not, for that matter, with complete success. Its connection with events in other parts of the world, primarily in
Vietnam, is also bound to come to mind.

We have not let ourselves be deflected, either by cross-
fire from abroad or by a lack of understanding in our own
country, from seeking an objective dialogue with the Soviet
Union. I will not be made to deviate from this goal, nor shall
I let myself be deflected from energetically continuing a conversation, initiated with so much difficulty, as purposefully
and as intensively as possible. It is well known that big advances cannot be achieved swiftly. The terrain must be prepared, and for that there must be favorable circumstances and
necessary intervals of time.

It remains our sincere desire to bring about an understanding with the Soviet Union by means of practical cooperation and an exchange of political opinions.

12

THE POLICY
OF DÉTENTE:
MENDING THE BRIDGE
BETWEEN EASTERN
AND WESTERN EUROPE

Accommodation with our Eastern neighbors is a high-priority aim of German foreign policy. We wish to improve our economic and cultural relations and also to initiate diplomatic relations with them wherever circumstances make this possible. .

At the same time, we know that a comprehensive accommodation will be reached only after West and East come to an understanding about the foundations of an enduring peace order. We can approach this goal only step by step, in a long-drawn-out process of détente, that is, by means of mutual rapprochement, understanding, and cooperation in all areas of interstate relations. The establishment of diplomatic relations is a means to the attainment of this goal, not an end in itself.

Our policy with respect to Eastern Europe—this must be emphasized again and again—cannot be separated from the shaping of our relationship to the Soviet Union.

The development of our relations with the other countries of Eastern Europe should supplement the development of our relationship to the Soviet Union, not run counter to it. The internal German accommodation is also closely related to our policy on Eastern Europe. We have made it clear that our readiness for a détente includes the German Democratic Republic. This has nothing to do with the surrender of vital interests.

The primary goal of our policy on Eastern Europe is to arouse confidence and eliminate distrust. As we once had to do in the West, we must now, under more difficult preconditions, pay off the mortgages of the past in the East. Our Eastern policy, starting from the given circumstances of today, is intended to help to overcome the division of Europe. Consequently we are particularly concerned with demonstrating the peaceable nature of our means and ends. Statements renouncing the use of force can contribute to this.

In January 1967 we established diplomatic relations with Rumania on the occasion of Foreign Minister Manescu's visit. About the same time, East Berlin and Warsaw, supported by Moscow, succeeded in hampering our conversations concerning the establishment of diplomatic relations with other Eastern European states. The conclusion of the friendship treaties of East Berlin with Poland, Czechoslovakia, Hungary, and Bulgaria does not, to be sure, bar the initiation of diplomatic relations with us, but it means a postponement of the course of normalization.

German policy with respect to Eastern Europe nevertheless showed a positive balance at the beginning of 1968. After the exchange of trade representations with Czechoslovakia, we now figure in all Eastern European states except Albania. We are the most important Western trading partner there; nor are all possibilities of economic cooperation exhausted.

E

Furthermore, cultural exchange with most of our neighboring Eastern states is growing; for example, the Federal Republic publishes by far more Eastern European literature than any other Western country.

In a number of capitals there is, as we know, a deep-lying desire for political talks and the readiness to normalize relations and to improve their content, but in East Berlin, Warsaw, and Moscow, especially, attempts are being made to block further progress toward improved relations. The influence of East Berlin and its capacities for working against our policy are obvious. The trend in certain European states toward greater freedom of movement vis-à-vis the West, including the Federal Republic of Germany, conflicts with certain economic and military bonds. The common ideology and the will to self-preservation of the Communist regimes are links that are still further strengthened by the friendship treaties of the German Democratic Republic with Poland, Czechoslovakia, Hungary, and Bulgaria. East Berlin also seems to have achieved a certain success with the argument that our policy on Eastern Europe is intended to isolate East Berlin.

In speaking of a positive interim balance at the beginning of 1968, nevertheless, I have in mind the following: First, we have found a great deal of agreement with our policy in the West and in the Third World. Second, some de facto advances have been made. Third, it can be said without hesitation that although there may be setbacks the development as a whole will proceed in the direction of multiplied contacts and improved relations.

It can be stated that an important result of our endeavors and of the support of our friends is that no one can be believed any longer who maintains that the Federal Republic of Germany is a mischief-maker or an obstacle to détente.

Here we are in the midst of a genuine change of climate. The accusations that the Federal government is preparing an act of aggression, that it is imperialistic, that it is jeopardizing the peace, and similar remarks—all such charges go into a vacuum. Anyone who puts them forward only becomes unbelievable.

We have never thought we could carry on an active policy on the East and a successful policy of détente at the price of an alienation from the West. Anyone who in foreign policy thinks in terms of the pendulum stroke misunderstands both its own laws and—in our case—the position of Germany. It was also erroneous to interpret the decision of the Federal Republic in favor of Western democracy as a decision against Central and Eastern Europe. I said in this connection that in foreign policy there were for me no spoiled darlings, no favorite children, and no stepchildren, but only the vital interests of the state and the nation, especially, however, the interest of securing the peace. Our Western allies have been urging us—rightly—over and over again to contribute to this détente during the past years.

At this point I would like to thank those of my European colleagues who in their conversations with Eastern European governments have shown so much understanding in their support of our endeavors to improve our relationship to these countries. I am thinking here of the foreign ministers of the Scandinavian countries and of the Benelux states and equally of the support of the French, the British, the Italian, and the Turkish foreign ministers. We are confident that the explanation of our policy of peace and détente by representatives of countries friendly to us will contribute to a deepening of the understanding of our sincere efforts in the Eastern European capitals.

The initiation of diplomatic relations with Rumania was

an important step, but both sides were obliged to put up with a good deal of criticism. In Germany some people asked why this step had not been taken sooner. Others spoke of a blunder on the part of Germany's Eastern policy because Rumania has remained an individual case. Mistaking the real state of affairs, such critics seem to have been expecting a chain reaction and were baffled when it failed to come about. Because it would be a mistake to let the understanding of our long-term policy be distorted by the ebb and flow of day-to-day political obstacles, my answer to those critics was that anyone who has waited years will be able to be patient a little while longer. From the very outset our calculations were founded on lengthy intervals of time. We are not putting any pressure on anyone, and we shall not let pressure be applied to ourselves. We have patience and confidence, an ability to act, and a long breath.

After ambassadors were exchanged with Rumania in the summer of 1967, a German-Rumanian accord was signed at the beginning of August for cooperation in technical and scientific domains. This accord was followed by negotiations for deepening economic relations. The conversations I conducted in August 1967 in Bucharest and at the Black Sea— the latter with the party head, Nicolae Ceaucescu, who has since become President—initiated an untrammeled political dialogue that can be of service to other countries as well. This is an example of a realistic kind of cooperation that pushes solid bridges far beyond the differences of political conceptions.

The agreement on goods and payments exchange and on the exchange of trade delegations between Czechoslovakia and the Federal Republic of Germany in the summer of 1967 was also an interim result of more than ephemeral importance. The initiation of these official relations was particularly important because Czechoslovakia and the Federal Republic of Germany are direct neighbors.

In February 1968 the gap in the network of trade missions between the states of Eastern Europe and the Federal Republic of Germany was closed by the exchange with Czechoslovakia of missions provided with consular capacities. The agreement was the beginning of longer-range accords that will surely lead to normalization of the relationship between the two states.

Diplomatic relations between the Federal Republic of Germany and Yugoslavia were broken off at the end of 1957 because Belgrade recognized the German Democratic Republic. The present Federal administration declared that it was concerned with the restoration of diplomatic relations. We were quite clear in our minds about the special, uncommitted attitude of Communist-ruled Yugoslavia. We thought we were aware of the conditions under which its relationship to the Soviet Union, which for years had been so tense, had again been normalized. But above all we were concerned with being able to work together with this important member of the European community of states in a policy of détente and in the perspective of a European peace order.

During the period in which there were no ambassadors the de facto links—economic, cultural, touristic—suffered surprisingly little damage, but both sides had an interest in improving what was already on hand. Because neither side set up any preconditions, by the beginning of 1968 there were no real difficulties in resuming diplomatic relations between Bonn and Belgrade. The exchange of ambassadors was no reason for either side to feel triumphant, but it was more than a merely encouraging sign. The domestic reaction in

Germany showed that our population does not hold much with dogmas and formulas that motivated a policy of limited duration, that were mere accessories unable to withstand the course of evolution.

We had the impression that the governments of Hungary and Bulgaria—as well as that of Czechoslovakia—were concerned with normalization, that is, with the resumption of diplomatic relations. However, these governments thought it correct, or timely, to take into account the demands of East Berlin and of others. We respected their position and made it clear that in the interim we would work together to improve de facto relations within the framework of what was possible.

Official Poland assumed an attitude toward our policy of détente that seemed to be irreconcilable. Although the Federal government gave vigorous emphasis to its desire for reconciliation, the Warsaw regime seemed uninterested in any talks. I find it regrettable that it still remains impossible to improve German-Polish relations. Our stated understanding for the Polish people's desire to live within secure boundaries has been dictated by our wish for reconciliation. We have said with honesty that, in view of our position, border questions can be decided only in a peace treaty. In our opinion, however, there is no sensible reason not to improve bilateral relations and begin a serious German-Polish conversation. I should like to reaffirm here my clear conviction that the reconciliation of Poles and Germans will someday have the same historical importance as the friendship between Germany and France.

The interest of the Eastern European states in cooperating with us rests to a large extent on a desire to make economic progress and to participate in Western technology. Economics, therefore, remains for the foreseeable future an especially important element of our policy on Eastern Europe. We should like to expand the economic exchange with the Eastern European states and as far as possible bring about a balancing of exports and imports. Such an exchange would demand a liberal trade policy vis-à-vis the East on the part of the European Economic Community. Wherever for structural reasons no leveling off of trade balances is possible, even when the liberalization is expanded, the granting of long-term credits should be considered. Even though we may take a soberer view of the prospects of "cooperation" than a number of Eastern European governments that have exaggerated expectations of it, nevertheless we ought to examine such projects without prejudice and to evolve constructive solutions.

The cultural exchange, especially where it leads to human and scientific encounters, is of use to all the states participating. We must realize, to be sure, that the possibilities of spreading and receiving information are not the same in Germany and in Eastern Europe. Cultural projects of our own, by means of which we can have an enlightening effect in Eastern Europe, are important and desirable.

We do not try to force political contacts, but we make use of them wherever the occasion offers. The inclination toward such contacts will increase in Eastern Europe insofar as there is an acceptance of the fact that the Federal Republic of Germany cannot be eliminated from the process of détente in Europe. We must, accordingly, work toward objective progress with tact and sobriety.

Détente is not possible if only one side is prepared to get rid of tensions, and we have made practical, concrete suggestions, supported by the Atlantic alliance, for normalizing our relationship to the Soviet Union and the Eastern European states. The present Federal administration is carrying on an unmistakable, consistent policy:

> It has said clearly and concisely that it well understands the Polish demand to live on its own state territory with secure boundaries and regards the reconciliation with Poland as an important part of the European peace order.
>
> This administration has also said distinctly that the Munich agreement came into being under the threat of force; it is no longer valid.
>
> This government has convincingly indicated that the Federal Republic of Germany is not aiming at the possession of atomic weapons or at the power to dispose of such weapons.
>
> This government is not two-tongued: it speaks the same language everywhere.

Among our people it is known with great certainty that we shall not attain a real accommodation until peace, understanding, cooperation, reconciliation, and—yes, I hope, one day—friendship as well prevail, not only in the West but also between Germany and its neighbors in the East.

I know how painful the road will be, but I am firmly convinced that we shall make progress along it. Our Eastern policy has not frozen, nor does it suffer from what has been so frighteningly referred to as the compulsion to success. The nations and the governments of Eastern Europe ought to realize that the German government would be behaving irresponsibly if it agreed to and promised more than it could stand for in the eyes of its own people and hold to in the future. As it is sometimes said in Eastern Europe that such new ideas were those of the Federal Foreign Minister only, I want to stress that they are the joint opinion of the Chancellor and the Vice Chancellor who is also the Foreign

Minister; they are the policy of the German Federal Government.

In the government statement of December 13, 1966, we stated that we were offering to each of the states in Eastern Europe, including the Soviet Union, an exchange of solemn statements renouncing the use of force. With respect to the German Democratic Republic and to the Warsaw pact, we added that we were ready to encompass, also, the thorny question of divided Germany.

The rulers in the other part of Germany have allowed themselves a deplorable step backward since the first months of 1966. At that time it was thought to be possible to achieve for the citizens of the German Democratic Republic, in their connection with us, at least some humanitarian relief. As mayor of Berlin I had to struggle for the modest passes to cross the borders, not only with the Communists in the East but also against the lack of understanding in the West. There was no longer any need for this dissipation of energies, but meanwhile the East Berlin authorities had decided on an isolation that was to be as thoroughgoing as possible. I am certain, however, that Walter Ulbricht and his people will not be able to sustain their policy of cantankerousness, sabotage, and general querulousness. In the Eastern European states and in the other part of Germany the pressure for exchange will become greater and greater in the years before us—in science, in economics, in technology. Anyone who seals himself off, who isolates himself, is setting himself against the mainstream of our times.

Although there are encouraging signs, on the other hand there is the persistent effort of some leaders—primarily, though not only in East Berlin—to fix their allies on a policy whose goal is to stop or at least to hamper a détente with the Federal Republic of Germany. These circles have far-

E*

reaching aims. They want NATO to be dissolved and the Americans to vanish from Europe. The possibility is not to be excluded that this political orientation will prevail in the Communist-ruled part of Europe—though, to be sure, for how long remains open.

From the very outset we were bound to reckon with opposition to any activation of our policy on Eastern Europe. The fact that such opposition came primarily from East Berlin was also not surprising. We weathered lively diplomatic and propagandistic activity. Attempts were made to bridge over differences of opinion among the Communist states with respect to the German policy of détente. Sanction was given to the Rumanian interpretation of the Bucharest statement of July 1966, according to which "formalizing" was not yet synonymous with "normalizing" of relations. At the same time friendship treaties were concluded between East Berlin and Prague, Warsaw, Budapest, and Sofia whose essential goal seemed to be to prove solidarity between them and the Communist-ruled part of Germany. In this way the German Democratic Republic was included in the bilateral network of treaties of the Warsaw pact. To what extent the Eastern European states allow themselves to be bound by these treaties vis-à-vis the Federal Republic of Germany remains subject to be sure, to their interpretation, hence to their political decision.

The Federal Republic will not be stopped in its efforts to go on striving for regulated, normal relations with the states of Eastern Europe. I do not see the negative reactions we have had to encounter as final. In the Eastern bloc, as well as in the Soviet Union itself, there are enough authoritative persons who know that the problems touching us both cannot be dismissed from the world by gruff statements. In February 1967, in the Deutschland hall in Berlin, I spoke of the day when no one would be surprised any longer at the emergence of cooperation, confidence, and even friendship not only between direct neighbors but also between Germany and the Soviet Union. At that time some people thought this remark was wholly novel. In reality what was and is at issue is nothing but the fact that the Federal government—and together with it the overwhelming majority of our people—simply want good and friendly relations with all nations. It is useful and necessary to repeat this from time to time.

We shall reach the stage in which it will be even more obvious than it is today that whether the détente in Europe can be promoted by practical progress, agreements, or accords will depend on the good will of the leaders of the Eastern European powers—and not on the attitude of the Federal Republic. What is a reality is that the Federal government is ready for this détente, that it is ready to be taken at its word.

I will not allow myself to be deflected from a path I regard as the right one, either by setbacks or by disappointments. We must cling to the goal of a reconciliation with our neighbors in the East, for otherwise there can be no enduring peace. In all this internal German relations, the relationship to East Berlin, must not be viewed in isolation. In reality there is a threefold aim in our policy on the East: improved relations with the Soviet Union, normal relations with the Eastern European states, and a *modus vivendi* between the two parts of Germany. And that aim will be realized or not be realized, will be promoted or jeopardized, by the developments in Europe as a whole and in the world at large.

The question of the future of Germany and of the position of Germans in Europe is the question of an enduring

European peace order. Only in a peacefully ordered Europe, which has succeeded in building a bridge between East and West and in which nations as equals among equals will vie with each other for peace, justice, and prosperity, will the past be overcome in a positive way.

The policy of the German government rests on the expectation and the hope that we can create a basis for common interests in Europe while mutually respecting differing social orders. The geographical situation of the German people gives us a special responsibility for this. For centuries Germany was a bridge between East and West. We are striving to build anew the shattered bridge, better, sturdier, and more reliable. Such a task can be performed only in an intimate and trusting collaboration with our friends and neighbors.

During the years prior to the formation of the present administration Bonn was encouraged by its allies to take up a less doctrinaire and a more self-confident attitude. Today I can say that we shall not let ourselves be shaken on our course of a consistent policy of détente, free of illusions.

13

THE
STATUS QUO,
OR THE DIFFICULTY
OF THE "REALITIES"

The Federal Republic of Germany has no territorial demands. What it wants is that the status quo of an insecure peace become a secure peace order. The present situation in Europe is the result of World War II. It is a reality that has been consolidated by postwar development and has remained unchanged for two decades. Hardly anyone can refuse to acknowledge this.

If, however, we are requested to recognize *all* the realities that have been created by World War II as the first step toward a détente, something else is being demanded. What is then at issue is the renunciation of every attempt to overcome by peaceful means the unnatural condition of the division of Germany and of the split within Europe. But that would mean a renunciation of common sense.

I never forget in all this that it was Hitler's "Greater Germany" that brought about such unspeakable misery, above all to Eastern Europe. And when present-day Germans let it be understood that they are contemplating the overcoming of the status quo they easily lay themselves open to a malicious misunderstanding. We must be unyielding in our efforts to clear up that misunderstanding.

What is at issue in this peaceful overcoming of the status quo? First of all, the overcoming of the military confrontation. What is at issue is a compatible Europe that will work together in as friendly a way as possible. What is at issue is the keeping open of a path on which the Germans— if it is their freely expressed will—can find a way to each other and live with each other.

It therefore is not a question of Germans putting forward territorial claims. The borders of 1937, prior to the annexations by Hitler, must be regarded as a legal starting point for negotiations aimed at a peace treaty and also as a sequel to the Potsdam Conference.

There is just as little question of the "incorporation" of the other part of Germany in the Federal Republic. Such ideas are outmoded even for those who once clung to them.

The transformation of the present status quo toward European cooperation and a just solution of the German question will take time. No advance can be made merely through impatient insistence. To that extent we have a clear view of the realities. And it is also a reality that we are striving toward this goal by exclusively peaceful means.

One cannot wish to force into a fixed form a process that to human reckoning must last a long time. Aside from that no one would be running a risk if he renounced any maximalist claims. It is true that the East Berlin government may take a different view of this. For it a policy of détente may be the greatest challenge conceivable. But it is very certain that this does not hold true for our Eastern European neighbors. Nor do I believe that for reasons of a false solidarity they will allow themselves to be barred by East Berlin from the path toward a European peace order. They have no need to fear a rapprochement of both parts of Germany.

Moreover, in more than one place during the past few years the question has been raised as to why it is not enough for Poland to have its boundaries recognized by the German Democratic Republic. In the official opinion of Warsaw the two German states are meant to continue. But in that case there is no border between the Federal Republic and Poland. Yet there seems to be a feeling that there may be changes in "the German question."

If the Federal Republic were to speak bindingly on behalf of all Germany, then Poland would still have no need to fear any forcible change of its boundaries. We do not feel legitimated to anticipate decisions of a future all-German Government and the settlement in a peace treaty, but we can respect and recognize the Oder-Neisse-line until such a peace settlement is concluded.

Such an attitude is inspired by the German desire for reconciliation with Poland even before a peace treaty is signed. Nobody thinks in terms of a new expulsion. It is a fact that 40 per cent of the people living in those areas have been born there.

Statements of this kind do not imply renunciation of legal titles. They simply take into account that legal titles do not in themselves constitute a claim to their realization. We know that the Oder-Neisse-line will continue to exist as long as there is a Federal Republic of Germany. It may sound surprising, but the Federal Republic has never claimed for herself the areas beyond the Oder-Neisse-line. It has never demanded that a strip of Federal territory be inserted between Poland and the German Democratic Republic. That is why it can respect and recognize the present Western frontier of Poland without, in doing so, taking anything away from the expellees or robbing the future Germany.

It would be hypocritical to pass in silence over a fact of which everybody is aware: If, in the course of a comprehensive peace settlement, the present situation were to be modified, such modification could never be agreed upon without the consent of the Polish people. Once the mutual renunciation of force which we have offered were declared, Poland could feel safe in its present frontiers. That is the clear and unequivocal meaning of our policy. That is the implication of the relevant wording of our government statement of December 13, 1966.

This stand illustrates a principle of our foreign policy that some people in the East tenaciously mask: What we hope for from the process of détente and rapprochement, the peaceful overcoming of the status quo and an honorable accommodation of interests, is not meant to be accomplished against the will of the nations participating but with their assent. And when I speak of the nations participating I also mean, of course, those countrymen of ours who are separated from us and who also have a will that must not be disregarded.

It is strange that so sober a word as "realities" can be so misunderstood and so wrangled over. What we are experiencing nowadays is the determination of certain Communists to turn all dialectic topsy-turvy and to conduct themselves as though world history would allow itself at some given point simply to be laid down in a fixed form in writing. We see still others sticking their heads into the sand.

In foreign policy a realist without imagination is a simpleton. But anyone involved in foreign policy who is not a realist is a dreamer. Not a day goes by that does not give rise to new realities, and anyone who believes that all present-day realities can be frozen for all eternity is a reactionary fool petrified to the point of utter rigidity.

In August 1967, during my visit to Rumania, I had some instructive experiences—I became acquainted with a beautiful country and encountered agreeable people. Moreover the comments made in Germany on the occasion of a table talk in Bucharest were illuminating. On the evening of August 3 I said in Bucharest:

> As for the great questions of our time, we agree that the maintenance and consolidation of world peace unequivocally deserve top priority. You have spoken, with a frankness we are able to appreciate, of the ties of your country. Well, the Federal Republic of Germany has its own self-chosen commitments in the Atlantic alliance and in the European communities. But our country, like your own, wants manifold collaboration and strives toward a comprehensive cooperation, in Europe especially.
>
> We also agree that in the problem of European security we must take as a starting point the prevailing realities, and that all states, regardless of size, have tasks of uniform importance in the realization of a European peace order. This also holds for both political societies that are in existence at present on German soil.
>
> For all of us the issue must be: to take away from people the feeling of insecurity and the fear of war.

It is true that the phrase "both political societies" was not in my manuscript, but that I consciously, under the impression of my conversation with my hosts, inserted it. That made it no less important. The following evening I made an equally conscious addition:

> Our policy is directed at everyone and against no one. It is aimed at bringing union and not separation. It seeks a just accommodation in Europe and it is also prepared to make

sacrifices. The sole means it makes use of is the power of persuasion; it has renounced force.

My government would like to work toward an improvement of the present situation in Europe, together with all the states concerned. There can, after all, be nothing reprehensible in trying to shape the world in a more sensible and a more just way! And there can, after all, be nothing sensible in taking the condition of the division of Europe and of my own country, and the military confrontation of heavily armed blocs, as history's final word!

We have no illusions. We are completely aware of the real facts of the situation. It is only that we regard it as the task, indeed the duty, of our policy to contribute with all our strength to overcoming the division of Europe and of Germany. For this we look into the future and endeavor to learn from the past. We are no fantasts, but we would like to help Europe to grow together again instead of drifting further apart.

We must start from the status quo. What else is there to start from? But it would be against nature and against reason to renounce any desire for future development. We must see the given circumstances without any blinders and without any wishful ideas alien to reality. And we must wish to change and improve the present-day facts in such a way that tension will give way to peace. This can only be done without force, that is, only in agreement with all those concerned.

We wish to eliminate the source of mischief—the division of Germany—by means of peaceful understanding and once again to give to our own people their peace with themselves and with the world. We wish—to quote my friend Herbert Wehner, the Federal Minister for all-German Affairs—to make things looser, not harder; to bridge over trenches, not deepen them.

Nothing would be more false than the assumption that we have lately come to believe in an isolated solution of the German questions. What is actually at issue is that perspective that leads beyond the reduction of tensions and beyond the banning of the danger of war, beyond a system of security to an enduring and just peace order. At the same time, we realize that the German problem can be solved only in connection with a general European settlement and can be advanced only in a situation of accommodation between East and West. We are not making our policy of détente dependent on any progress with respect to the question of Germany.

In the other part of our country, in the German Democratic Republic, a political system rules that does not meet with our approval, that we reject; but it exists and rules. We want the common substance of a common nation to persist not only in the memory of man. We want to stand by each other, we want the barriers to be lowered—not least of all out of a feeling of responsibility for peace in Europe.

Our point of view regarding the territory that calls itself the German Democratic Republic has been determined by two basic factors. The first factor is that in this area there live 17 million Germans who are our countrymen and who have undeservedly suffered a more difficult fate; who have not lost the war any *more* than those of us in the Federal Republic; for whose fate we feel and assume an obligation and a responsibility; with whom we wish to maintain contacts or create new ones; whose lives we wish to make easier, as far as that is in our power.

The second factor is based on our resolve not to allow

any recognition under international law to be given to the regime that has been set up in this territory—because it does not represent the will of the people, because without Soviet troops it could not have maintained itself, because it prevents the exercise of the right of self-determination, because it is hampering the solution of the German question.

Nevertheless, what is at issue is not the question of who recognizes and who does not recognize whom. What is at issue are the people and peace. We have good grounds for not letting the present-day situation be sanctioned under international law and for not recognizing the other part of Germany as a foreign country. We have made positive suggestions as to how a great deal might be improved if one put aside those points on which no agreement can be reached and if one concentrated on areas of common interest. I think that responsible leaders on the other side, too, under the other political system, will in the long run have to recognize what is expected from Germans in both parts of Germany— that is, to begin living next to each other within our nation in a peaceful way, to have compatible relations with each other, not to impose needless burdens on people, and not to jeopardize the peace in Europe, but to make it more secure.

If the leadership in East Berlin is afraid of finding itself isolated, its fear must be ascribed to its own policy, which by its dogmatic, didactic manner and attempts to speak for its allies in the Warsaw pact and to forbid or make difficult their establishing diplomatic relations with us, ultimately isolates only itself.

We do not desire any such isolation; on the contrary, we are striving to have this area take part in the process of European détente. In a surrounding world that is seeking to overcome the barriers between states, our countrymen in the other part of Germany should not be forced to live as the only ones who are sealed off. Because of this we submitted to East Berlin, in April 1966, sixteen suggestions for an extension of intra-German contacts that can be implemented without either side demanding that the other give up its political standpoint. For we are of the opinion that there are many problems that might be solved within Germany, too, regardless of the great differences of our political systems and points of view.

There was a tempestuous discussion when the Federal Chancellor took cognizance of a letter from Prime Minister Stoph in East Berlin. I could find nothing sensational in this. After the Federal government had made its statement on Germany and the chairman of the Social Democratic Party of Germany had submitted this document, together with a supplementary statement, to the seventh party convention of the Socialist Unity Party (of the German Democratic Republic) such a step was bound to be taken into account. If one undertakes a political sally one must realize that it will have consequences. In any case it is reasonable to read the letters that come in and to answer them. Once upon a time this might not have been so; now it is. What was and is at stake is the serious attempt to make some progress in the German question in the interest of people and of peace. The Federal government is not setting forth its ideas as propagandistic theses with the preconceived intention of eluding the expected consequences. We mean what we say.

An exchange of opinions is not, to be sure, an independent goal. One must know what is worth talking about. Putting up one's maximal demands does not lead far. The opposite side also knows that, and they ought to ponder on the preconditions of intra-German progress. Over there they speak of a desirable cementing of the status quo. What serves to overcome the status quo is called revanchism;

what leaves it untouched is called a love of peace. Such primitive clichés do not fit into the realities of today. Politics must endeavor to make life easier for people in a divided country instead of needlessly making it more difficult for them.

We are not giving away anything when we answer letters from East Berlin. And if deputies of both political orders were to speak with each other, no shrines would be surrendered. We know what we are, what we represent, where we have our mandate from, and what constitutes our obligation to the other part of the German people.

This has absolutely nothing whatever to do with any arrogant claim to speak for all Germany. It is precisely our political and ethical obligation that gives rise to a broad arena for discussions of how the coexistence of Germans in East and West can be normalized. The Federal government has suggested a whole catalog of themes that will allow itself to be expanded and transmuted. Anyone who merely counterposes maximal demands is swimming against the mainstream of the times. He will be able to convince no one, in Germany or abroad.

Vis-à-vis the chairman of the Council of Ministers, Mr. Stoph, Federal Chancellor Kiesinger emphasized that as long as fundamental differences of opinion make any solution of the German question impossible, it is necessary, in the interest of the nation, of peace, and of détente, to come to some intra-German agreements that will facilitate the human, economic, and cultural bonds between Germans in both parts of our country. We champion the welfare of countrymen who are living under a regime they never sought. However much the administrators of political power on the other side bar themselves off they will not, in the long run, be able to avoid taking the only path on which respect and esteem are to be won. To say it clearly and in one sentence, the more freedom the East Berlin regime can let people have, the more recognition and approval it can find in the world at large.

Regardless of the still negative attitude of the authorities in East Berlin, the Federal government will continue its endeavors to loosen up the intra-German situation. The détente in Europe must, we are convinced, encompass the détente in Germany.

It cannot be my intention to draw a propagandistic caricature of the Communist-ruled part of my fatherland. There can be no doubt that substantial advances have been made there, for example, in economic reconstruction. This was no easy matter for our countrymen there.

They are understandably proud of what has been achieved. Nevertheless, it cannot be denied that the wall is standing in Berlin, the death strip stretches from the Baltic Sea to the border of Czechoslovakia, and we cannot cut off our gaze from the injustice or grow accustomed to it or come to terms with it.

Just because of this we shall attempt to make complete use of the politically possible framework of intra-German contacts so that both parts of our people will not drift further away from each other. We are striving toward a better neighborliness in Germany that will permit increasingly far-reaching solutions of the question of Germany. In the long run the Communist leaders in East Berlin will be less able to evade our stubborn and unillusioned endeavors the more our friends in Europe keep in mind the special situation of Germany and its European effects.

Anyone who speaks of a détente in Europe must not do so as though there were no Communist-ruled part of Germany—there is. And what we must accept—not as superfluous polemics but as a fact—is that East Berlin hitherto has evaded all efforts on behalf of a détente by means of either pretexts or unfulfillable demands. In this connection one should recall how they evaded our offer to exchange speakers between the two parts of Germany. I am also thinking of the monstrous difficulties that the East Berlin regime made in the conversations about passes, a matter that is inconsequential in comparison with the questions that must be settled and yet is nevertheless so important for the people affected. There are three decisive points at issue:

First, the continued responsibility under international law of the four powers to solve the German question. This is an important position when it is not made a mere screen behind which to hide one's own inactivity or to deny the political responsibility of the Germans. Moreover, it must be soberly recognized that the Soviet Union shows little inclination to live up to this responsibility, with the sole exception of what is called in Moscow the questions of European security. To be sure, one must realize that the three Western powers have not always been able to achieve any genuine agreement, either, with respect to the German questions. One must recognize these facts in speaking of the responsibility of the four powers.

The second point has to do with the "right to speak for all Germany." Here it is correct, of course, to say that the Federal Republic of Germany is the state in which Germans can freely express their will and in which a government at work for the state has been legitimized by the will of the population. In accordance with the constitution this gives rise to the duty of speaking up for those Germans who are forbidden to give free expression to their will. This political and ethical obligation cannot be exercised in a rigid way. It must take into account the real situation in Germany as well as changes in world affairs. The representatives of Communist Germany must not indirectly determine, either, where the Federal Republic of Germany has to pull down its flag.

The third point concerns nonrecognition. It is completely clear that the Federal Republic cannot regard the regime in the other part of Germany as democratically and legally legitimized. But we ought not spin, or let someone else spin, a cord out of this that can also bind ourselves. What we primarily refuse to recognize is that the other part of Germany is a foreign country for us. Intra-German settlements are not an object for politics with respect to foreign states. Otherwise the de facto split would be cemented as a matter of international law and thus made very nearly irreparable.

The Federal government does not claim the exercise of any sovereignty for German territories outside the area of validity of its constitution. It grants the authorities in the other part of Germany those functions inherent in the power that has been transferred to them. It does not constitute part of our policy to exclude that part of the German people that is ruled by East Berlin from international exchanges in the areas of trade, culture, and other aspects of life. Under international law, however, recognition must not be granted to the regime in East Berlin because for us the German Democratic Republic is not a foreign country.

It remains a fact that the government in the other part of Germany was never legitimized by the people. It is also a fact that the Geneva four-power conferences in 1955 and 1959 foundered on the intransigence of the Soviets. Yet, in the course of twenty years, facts have developed that cannot be denied. They do not vanish through the mere repetition of old demands. The political byplay of the past few years has not brought us the right of self-determination. I have no intention of indulging in speculation as to what might have happened if . . . Most people have long since learned that quarrel about that is fruitless.

During these past two decades it has certainly become increasingly difficult to solve the German question; in this area, too, "prices" have been rising steadily. It may be decisive for the future of democracy in our country that our nation not be left to believe in a miracle-to-come, a belief which one day would be frustrated or even turn into the bitter feeling that our friends have let us down. International dogmatism or sulkiness may be an easy path to tread, but it will not be successful. Whether we like it or loathe it, the world does hardly feel that it owes us something. This is a fact, though not always a pleasant one.

It is obvious, twenty-three years after the war, that German interests cannot be protected if one confines oneself to merely maintaining a legal position. An attitude of mere defensiveness has, rather, facilitated the consolidation of the ruling system in the other part of Germany. The starting point for any attainment of our general German objectives in accordance with the principle of self-determination has not improved during the past few years but has worsened. If we want to change the facts, we must start out from the facts of the present day. In this we are not so conservative as those Communists who pretend to believe they can perpetuate a status quo of division and of the building up of military power in a way that is both undialectical and contrary to history.

On the other hand we can be sure that in the other part of Germany this belief is not shared by everyone even in the leading institutions of the Socialist Unity Party. There, too, there are debates. They are long drawn out and often painful. Nor can they be shortened by our simply deciding, as many in the grip of illusions demand of us, that Ulbricht must become more reasonable.

During 1967 more or less convulsive attempts were repeatedly made in East Berlin to move away from the concept of a single German nation. Positions were taken up that make a mockery of all reason. Some of the Socialist Unity Party leaders seem to have taken it into their heads that the 17 million Germans on the other side no longer have anything in common with us in the Federal Republic —no common past and of course no common future. If a substitute word for "German" had occurred to these overzealous people, they presumably would have introduced the new word at once. The Socialist Unity Party has meanwhile retreated from this extreme point; it has manifestly recognized it as dangerous for its own position. The people are not letting themselves be talked into the idea that there are two German nations.

Although the wish to construct an enduring European peace order is becoming stronger and more concrete in East and West, further attempts are being made in East Berlin to tear apart permanently a nation that has more than a thousand years of history behind it, an end that is counter not only to the will of the German people but also to the interests of the other European nations. This will be understood precisely in Poland, for there people realize that it has proved to be historically impossible to keep a nation divided over the long run. All nations have the right to live in unity and in a secure national domain. For our people, too, this is not an exaggerated demand, and the Federal government is going to attempt—by exclusively peaceful means—to attain this objective or come close to it. We have renounced force vis-à-vis everyone, as well as vis-à-vis the other part of Germany. We are prepared to prove this in any place and at any time and to proclaim it in a binding way. But no one can impute desires for revenge to us when we say that for us, the people of the state represented by the Federal Republic of Germany—and, I make a point of adding, for us, the Social Democratic Party of Germany—there is *one single* nation, not two. And that is no new reality, but an old one. One day it will be beyond question once again.

Until then we shall have to expend a great deal of effort to make it clear to the nations of Europe and to their governments that our policy aspires to security for all: security in the West and in the East, and security for the Germans, too. For us it goes without saying that this concept must encompass secure boundaries, as was clearly expressed in the government statement and in the policy based on it. In the Federal Republic there is no serious political figure who would want to contest the right of our neighbors to a secure national realm.

There remains in full view on the table of history what the ruling group of the Socialist Unity Party leadership would like to sweep under the carpet. The theme of the consolidation of peace, the theme of better neighborliness in the interest of people, the theme of normalization in the exchange—these themes and others remain on the agenda, even though at the moment they cannot be raised for negotiation.

We must look at the world as it is, not as it might have been, I said in Tutzing in July 1965. German responsibility for the solution of German questions has grown greater. This responsibility can only mobilize the interests of others if the security of peace is its primary goal. The world will have to turn its attention, after it has eliminated the danger in Southeast Asia, to the problem of establishing relations in Europe that are stable, that correspond to the will of the nations, and that thus entail the strongest conceivable consolidation of the peace. The German people can make a decisive contribution to peace. That is our will, and consequently we must attempt to solve the German problem.

A peace plan for Europe is the real target of our desire to implement the right of the German people to self-determination.

The policy of alliances has guaranteed the security of the Federal Republic, including the special Federal territory of West Berlin, and that is a good thing. Our security must not be jeopardized in any place and under any circumstances. But the security of the Federal Republic vis-à-vis an external danger does not automatically bring us any closer to German unity. The so-called politics of strength has proved to be politics based on illusions that are all too strong. Just as deceptive is the widespread hope that the Soviet monolith will collapse, bringing about the unity of Germany all by itself. Nor do defensive, merely anti-Communist magical formulas give any help.

If the Germans do not act, no progress will be made with respect to the German question. The Federal Republic will not evade the task of working toward a comprehensive peace settlement tirelessly and creatively. The preliminary labors for a peace treaty cannot be separated from the theme of the reunification of Germany. They have nothing to do with a surrender of juridical positions.

The rights and duties of the allies with respect to Germany as a whole cannot take the place of the rights and duties of the Germans with respect to Germany. We must not expect more from others than we ourselves are prepared to do and are capable of doing within the framework of what is possible. We need neither tranquilizers from our allies nor Cassandra outcries concerning their fidelity to treaties. We must, rather, be prepared to bear the greatest measure of responsibility for our own fate. We must and we wish to go on acting in concert with our allies, in order to achieve a just and enduring peace for us and for Europe.

I presented this course to the Dortmund party convention of June 1966, when I introduced the notion of neighborliness into the discusion. As Foreign Minister today I have not drawn back from that position. If one were to prefer a foreign word it would be *modus vivendi*—putting aside for the time being those political and juridical positions concerning which no agreement was possible. If Ulbricht and his people prefer isolation, nothing will move in the immediate future, but the cause itself does not thereby lose its rightfulness.

On the other hand, anyone who has been pursuing a policy of his own for many years should neither rejoice at nor be surprised by the fact that everything has become much more difficult.

Our people think more sensibly on many questions than many a person who plays himself up so gladly as the guardian of the holy grail of national interests. Recognizing realities, including disagreeable realities, and taking them into account for purposes of policy does not harm but rather benefit German interests. The German people can expect nothing from people whose whole wisdom is summed up by their seeing that something or other has been "surrendered" today and then the next day giving warnings of "irresponsible concessions." Suggestions of this kind have hampered sensible policies for far too long.

What was meant by the formulation of neighborliness is no longer a sensation today, but is the policy of the government. We have taken pains to see to it that the intra-German

discussion is conducted in a way that is different from before. In the part of Germany for which the Federal government is elected the argumentation is carried on objectively—
and if necessary with objective harshness. The Federal Republic is no longer considered abroad to be a state that is
sleeping through the great political movements of the world.
Our country used to be considered as hampering peaceful
evolution; that image has been changed quite basically. I was
able to observe this during my travels and in my conversations
with political persons from the East and the West. The
Federal Republic of Germany is no such obstacle. It represents its legitimate interests, and it promotes détente wherever and whenever it can. The future will show how important that effort is.

It is not the Federal Republic that runs the risk of ignor-
ing great political developments. This role has been taken
over with immense zeal by the commanders in East Berlin.
To be sure, they always limped somewhat behind developments, but now their reaction occasionally takes on grotesque
forms. They, who have always called on the Federal Republic to think "realistically," will presumably be the last
to take up a stand on the "new realities." This by no means
fills us with joy nor with the slightest tinge of triumph.

For several years Berlin has no longer been the crystallization point of dangerous international crises, and we have
every reason not to complain about that. Yet the situation
of the people in Berlin remains lamentable; they suffer more
than other Germans on account of the division, because those
who bear the responsibility for the German Democratic
Republic are sacrificing all conceivable human relief on the
altar of lifeless principles.

West Berlin is separated from the eastern part of the
city and from its environs by a border that with frightening

cynicism is called "modern." Its fortifications have become a sad attraction for the whole world. They serve no purpose other than keeping people from each other. Not even at Christmas—neither in 1966 nor in 1967—were there any passes for the Berliners. The attempt to secure agreements has been shattered by the obduracy of the officials in East Berlin. Instead of helping the people in divided Berlin, instead of permitting the separated families to reunite at least on holidays, they launched a malicious campaign against West Berlin. The leadership of the Socialist Unity Party raises groundless claims in its desire to alarm the population. At the same time, the Federal government and the Senate are accused of wanting to change the status of Berlin unilaterally.

As the German Foreign Minister, and also as a Berlin citizen and for many years the mayor of Berlin, I say that that attitude and that campaign are the opposite of a détente. Whoever now threatens to change the Berlin situation unilaterally counteracts all attempts to enhance peace in Europe.

The different views of the status of Berlin are well known. It is clear that they need be no obstacle to practical solutions and concrete improvements. The legal basis is the much-quoted four-power status, which has been frequently used as an excuse to oppose reasonable solutions and suggestions. It has been depleted and has petrified during the division, but it stands.

In West Berlin the occupation powers became protective powers in the very first postwar years. The relationship to them changed very quickly. They helped us and as a rule did not hamper our work. Not only the resistance to the blockade and the Khrushchev ultimatum, but the reconstruction, too, had the appearance of a splendid common undertaking. Nevertheless the fact remained that in West

Berlin it is the Three Powers that hold supreme sovereignty. This is, indeed, indispensable for the security of the city. The Federal government has not the smallest intention of experimenting with this situation. This has also always held true for the Berlin Senate and will, I am convinced, hold true for it in the future.

The Western powers did not manage to safeguard the unity of Berlin, that is, to make the four-power status effective, as was its real point, for Berlin as a whole. They and we together were unable to prevent the amputation of the city. But there is no sense in complaining about missed opportunities.

According to our own legal interpretation, which corresponds to the will of the population, West Berlin belongs to the Federal Republic of Germany. The de facto inclusion of West Berlin in our legal, economic, and currency system was not hindered by any allied reserved rights. On the contrary, this inclusion was laid down and brought about with the assent of the Three Powers. This de facto adherence is decisive for the viability of the city. It must not, accordingly, be interfered with.

Politically we used to formulate the interaction between allied and German law as follows: As much adherence and incorporation as possible without diminishing the position of the allies. There is no reason to subtract from this or to change it.

The legal concept of the Three Powers allows for only a conditional union between the Federal Republic and Berlin. It does not prompt the Federal government to raise a claim of sovereignty. This also derives from the reserved rights contained in the Bonn Treaty. It is no contradiction of this treaty—neither legal nor political—that the Federal government is obligated and authorized "to secure the representa-

F

tion of Berlin and of the population of Berlin externally."
The Federal government, in the external representation of
Berlin, has an obligation that does not diminish the rights of
the Three Powers and that is independent of the differing
interpretations of the legal position. Its obligation corresponds to its will and has always corresponded to the will,
also, of the population of Berlin. Practical agreements on this
basis are possible without touching the differing juridical
views.

These are realities; they are not altogether simple for us,
but we have come to terms with them. They are realities
that the Communists, too, must come to terms with. People
in the East must realize that the political status of Berlin
will not be changed unilaterally. As long as no satisfactory
solution has been found for the question of Germany with
the assent of the German people and of the powers concerned, Berlin cannot give up its status and the powers that
protect it. The Federal government is striving, on behalf of
Germany and thus on behalf of Berlin, for a solution within
the framework of a European peace order. There can be no
negotiations between Bonn and Moscow aimed at changing
the status of Berlin.

The paramount obligations of the Federal government
continue to be to do everything it can to keep alive and to
further the ties between West Germany and West Berlin;
not to weaken but to consolidate the position of Berlin in
the legal system, the financial constitution, and the economic
order of the Federal Republic of Germany; to make the
representation of Berlin in external politics and external
economics as secure as is indicated by the treaty agreements
with the Three Powers; to include Berlin in all attempts to
fortify the human, economic, and intellectual bonds between
both parts of Germany and to loosen up intra-German relations; and to give understanding and trusting support to the

Senate of Berlin without acting as its guardian or crippling its initiative.

For our part, we need not now engage in a full-fledged fight with the East over legal positions the outcome of which would be uncertain and might have consequences dangerous for all concerned. In accordance with our wishes, however, the existing positions must be maintained until the time comes for a comprehensive peace settlement in Europe and in Germany. Until then West Berlin must remain viable and, above all, must be strengthened economically.

There can no longer be any doubt that the Berlin economy is and must remain a part of the Western economy. The economy of Berlin must not be allowed to suffer as a result of its special position. It must, rather, be given the possibility of making use of its geographical situation. It is, for instance, quite unnatural for the rates of growth of the so-called "Eastern" businesses in West Germany to be higher than they are in Berlin. It goes without saying that what goes for the Western part of Germany also goes for Berlin: there is no secure perspective for our people if it does not succeed in bringing about an accommodation with the nations of the East, too.

Berlin can and will work together with us in our peace policy. The policy of détente pursued by the Federal government is a good policy for Berlin, too. The détente must not by-pass Berlin. Berlin must remain the barometer on which not only bad but good weather can be read.

There is no lack of preparedness on our part. It is precisely in Berlin that a first sign must be given as to whether the other side, too, is ready for a genuine understanding. It is the task of German policy to find the path to peace, to European security, and to a just peace order. Berlin has an indispensable role to play in this task, for Berlin holds a promise for the future of our people.

14

PERSPECTIVES
OF OUR EASTERN POLICY

Our foreign policy toward Eastern Europe is being carried out, as has been described, in two closely interconnected realms. It encompasses our relationship to the Soviet Union as well as our relationship to the countries east and southeast of Germany that are linked to the Soviet Union.

If this part of our foreign policy is to be called an Eastern policy, then the relativity of this concept should be pointed out. States like Poland and Czechoslovakia lie to the east of Germany, to be sure, but there are excellent geographical, historical, and cultural reasons for thinking of them as part of Central Europe or, more accurately, Eastern Central Europe.

There is a third realm that cannot be separated from our Eastern policy: the relationship to the other part of Germany. Here it is not a question of foreign policy in the real sense of the word, for in relationship to each other the two German regions are not foreign territory. The regime in East Berlin, however, is so tightly intermeshed with the group of states whose ruling power is the Soviet Union that an Eastern policy formulated without taking German questions into account would be unrealistic.

In all three realms our goals are the same: securing peace, reducing tensions, improving relations, and preparing contributions to a European peace order. While we have been coping with these goals, changes have taken place—especially since the formation of the present Federal government by the two great democratic parties—that are not merely of a gradual or formal nature. In expressing myself on the perspectives of this policy I shall lean on an article that I wrote for the American review *Foreign Affairs.*

It is often said in the East that our policy is a smokescreen behind which we are clinging all the more implacably to the "negation of realities," to the "politics of power," to the race for atomic weapons, and to the Cold War. This view is wrong. Of course there are some fundamental elements in our policy, as there are in that of every state, that will not let themselves be changed. Germany's policy, too, must be based on facts, the vital requirements of its people and a future stable peace order. We shall of course cling fast to these—and not, indeed, in our own interests alone but also in the interest of our allies and friends and in the interest of the principles of order that we are convinced must achieve recognition in international politics. But that has nothing to do with the above-mentioned reproaches that are cast at us by the propaganda of the East.

One reality is the division of Europe and the integration of its parts into the two heavily armed power blocs. This division runs through the continent and splits Germany. Consequently, one part of Germany has been drawn into the Western camp, the other, into the Eastern. This polarity, too, is a political reality, to be sure a perilous one. It is also artificial and unjust, for it does not permit a people to live as a nation according to its desires. We know, however, that this division will not vanish from one day to the next and that as far as can be foreseen will be overcome only in conjunction with a general improvement of East-West relations in

Europe. We must, accordingly, not only include the factor of time in our policy but also expend more effort on finding rules for the coexistence of both parts.

At the same time, we reject a German policy that would weaken the cohesion of the North Atlantic Treaty Organization or reduce the decisive participation of the United States in safeguarding the freedom of Europe. We are, on the contrary, convinced that we shall be improving our relationship to our allies if, with no illusions, we set our course by the realities and at the same time avoid even a shadow of ambiguity. A solid and enduring détente with the Soviet Union, which together with its allies spreads out over half the European continent, is quite impossible as long as the presence and the active participation of the other world power, America, does not establish a balance of power. A commitment of this sort will be indispensable for a European peace order, too.

Within the framework of these facts, which include a growing convergence within the European communities, there are, however, important changes to be noted. They are to be explained on the basis of the changed world situation and on the basis of the changed political landscape of the Federal Republic of Germany.

An improvement in the relationship between the two world powers has been noticeable for some years now— recognizable, perhaps, since the solution of the Cuban crisis, but above all as applied to Europe. This is certainly not yet synonymous with détente having worldwide effects. Such an assumption would be wishful thinking. We note, however, the American estimate that even with the present-day encumbrances on the American-Soviet relationship, attempts to bring about a détente are necessary, and not only in Southeast Asia. One can take as a starting point the fact that in

Europe we are no longer in a Cold War that might turn into a hot one at any moment. There are, to be sure, no guarantees against setbacks, but it seems justifiable to reckon, at least partially, with a mutual feeling of responsibility on the part of the world powers. Therefore, the fear of Europe to fall victim to a sudden violent clash has receded into the background.

This has brought about certain consequences in the Eastern as well as the Western camp, in the relations of the allies to each other, and between the systems of pacts on a bilateral as well as on a multilateral plane. There is no question at all here of only positive consequences, yet it is possible, nevertheless, to perceive that a process of progressive economic, cultural, political, and human relations has been launched. Neither nationalist thinking nor claims of hegemony that might issue from the world powers, either objectively or subjectively, have been able to stop the expansion of this process. Europe, indeed, Europe *as a whole,* is undergoing a historic transformation in the course of which ancient kinships are being discovered and new ones found. People are talking to each other again. Technical, economic, scientific, and intellectual communications are leading to a fruitful exchange and to a rising understanding for the situation and the interests of others. Political and propagandistic monologues are giving way to more and more dialogue, more and more listening to each other.

We Germans have no desire to constitute an obstacle to this development. Not only do we want to let this process run its course, but we should like to further it. We realize that it is not enough to announce one's peaceable intentions: one must actively strive to set afoot the organization of this peace. For this, what is needed is the renunciation of all forms of use or threat of force in international life. This attitude rests not only on the conviction that a war must never again start from German territory; it is the product of our own vital interests.

The Federal Republic would be drawn into any major military conflict between East and West. It would ineluctably be its first victim. Our people would cease to exist, for the concentration of troops, war equipment, and atomic means of annihilation on German soil is unprecedented throughout the world.

This danger has brought about a special concern on the part of the Federal Republic of Germany and a special obligation to strive tenaciously, even though without illusions, toward the reduction of mistrust and of tensions. This process can make no progress without the active collaboration of the two world powers, of the European states in the East and the West, and of both parts of Germany. And there exists for us a special responsibility toward the other part of Germany.

The German policy of détente must be conducted with resolution and patience. We must maintain our security, our partnership with the West, and our freedom. As part of this, to be sure, there must also be the knowledge that German policy has become more independent.

The Federal Republic has given many proofs of its reliability during the past two decades. It has allied itself so intimately with a group of European states that a process of integration and of the creation of supranational authorities has been set in motion that can no longer be reversed. We have consciously and resolutely chosen this path, not to undo history, which in fact is not possible, but rather to make a new beginning because we are aware of the past and of the responsibility that flows from it. Much of what once was considered essential to a "nation-state" and to a "national" policy—and which to many, seems indispensable even today—has been shed in the process. Thus we have, for instance, renounced national control over our armed forces.

In domestic policy we have shown, at the same time, that a democratic order has grown up among us that is strong enough to deal with extremist political phenomena in a democratic way.

We have learned from the past. We intend to prove ourselves to be a modern, trustworthy state. The conviction has spread even more strongly than before, during the months since the formation of the Great Coalition, that in the present world situation the Federal Republic possesses a special responsibility that parallels the interests of our friends and allies; it corresponds to the often expressed desire of the leading power in the Atlantic alliance, as well as to the thinking of our European allies. A policy of seesawing or balancing back and forth between East and West, by capitalizing on tensions, is now quite out of the question. The political relations, the historic facts, and the forces involved cast such a possibility back into the realm of the frivolous. Our policy implies close consultation with our allies, as well as the knowledge that we do not control interests that concern the Atlantic alliance and the European community as a whole.

On one fundamental issue the political objective has changed: The starting point in the capitals of our allies and in Bonn used to be that an accommodation with the Soviet Union, a bridging over of the power political conflict of interests in Central Europe, was unthinkable unless the problem of the division of Germany was solved first. This position gave rise to the demand that every step of the great powers toward each other, at least insofar as it was related to Eu-

F*

rope, be a step that at the same time counteracted the division of Germany. This was to prevent the division, the unsolved paramount problem of Europe, from being sanctioned and petrified. This idea remains correct, but the approach can no longer be to demand top priority for the reunification of Germany.

Our policy today recognizes the connection between European development and the German problem. It is concentrated on changing for the better the present-day status quo of mistrust, of tensions, and of conflicts. If it is to be successful, it must not be burdened with preconditions, neither from one side nor from the other, that constitute an anticipation of what actually has yet to be achieved. Thus, a long and painful road lies before us. In many places it has been piled high with debris that must be cleared away with patience and good will by *both* sides. The less one side is prepared to meet the other side halfway along this path, the more long-drawn-out will be the process of détente, of the real accommodation of interests, and of the establishment of a European peace order.

Our relationship to the leading power in the group of socialist states, the Soviet Union, is of crucial importance. This recognition is due to world political facts, to power relationships and to the interests in Eastern Europe. I therefore make the point that it is no more the goal, or even a collateral intention, of our Eastern policy to isolate East Berlin than it is to bring about or to exploit differences between the Soviet Union and its allies, even if that is asserted in the propaganda of the East.

We shall go on striving to improve our relations with the Soviet Union, which are very far from being as good as we would wish. We are trying, first of all, to get into conversations in those areas in which an understanding

might now be possible. There have also been initial prompt-
ings for a discussion of more complicated questions. One
day we hope—in accord with the United States and our
European allies—to be able to have a frank discussion of all
the problems between us and thus to take the first steps toward mastering them. It is our hope that reason and objectivity will one day triumph. We must demonstrate the
requisite patience.

We must recognize the fact that the Soviet Union is
linked to a series of other states by manifold ideological
and economic bonds and that the German Democratic Republic has been closely drawn into this field of force.

We should underrate these facts if we were to try to carry
on a policy of détente around East Berlin. The struggle for
a secure peace in Europe will not allow itself to be parceled
out, either regionally or substantially. We can also see this
in the political and military events in other parts of the
globe where we are not committed ourselves.

The other part of Germany is also a reality. The internal
German area, as constituted on the basis of the division, is to
a special degree our responsibility and our concern within
the framework of a more far-reaching policy of détente.
There we Germans have obligations and possibilities that
concern us more than other nations. Our policy signifies that
we are ready to regulate our relationship to this part of Germany differently from the way it has been regulated until
now.

We have made it clear, to be sure, that an international
recognition of this part of Germany, in which a quarter of
the German people lives, is impossible for this very reason.
Aside from this, we would in such a case take responsibility
for deciding a question whose solution does not depend on
ourselves alone. We are convinced that no other people sub-

jected to such a fate would behave any differently. This resolve on the part of the great majority of a people is also a political reality, as is just as well known in East Berlin. We hope that in East Berlin, too, the responsibility for the whole of the German people, so often stated there in a different sociopolitical environment, will never permit such a step that would run counter to history. No one can evade national responsibility. When we raise our voice in the behalf of the German people and give expression—as we know—to the opinion of the overwhelming majority of Germans in the Western as well as in the Eastern part of our country, we do not want to pose as tutor to our countrymen in the East. It is rather that we thereby give expression to the mutual desire to be joined together again.

Our present-day policy on Germany starts out from the fact that the termination of the division of Germany will be a process whose duration no one can predict. What we must do is what is possible now, or we shall succumb to wishful thinking or resignation. Both would be irresponsible, as it would also be, of course, to take the path of least resistance or to certify, against our conviction, democratic legitimation to the regime in the German Democratic Republic.

It is our present-day task to work for better neighborliness between the two parts of Germany. We want to lessen the tragedy of the division, under which many Germans are suffering bitterly. We want to maintain and strengthen the feeling of belonging together.

Hitherto these efforts have remained overwhelmingly onesided. In practice East Berlin has attempted to evade all collaboration for the reduction of existing tensions. It has, rather, set new demands and made their fulfillment a precondition for any kind of conversation. This conduct may be looked upon as an attempt to create for oneself a better negotiating position, but our experience leads us to assume that the East Berlin leaders are trying to evade all conversation, even when it is sought by us completely unencumbered by any preconditions. The only conclusion possible is that these leaders do not want to hear of any détente and still refuse to recognize the grand conjunctions that are at issue in Europe today and will be still more so tomorrow. In East Berlin ideas are being clung to that belong to the past. This immobility is bringing East Berlin into a situation that is in such contradiction to the realities that more and more difficulties keep cropping up more and more rapidly. East Berlin must constantly conjure up anew the solidarity of its allies. It must strive for the support of a policy that does not always correspond to the interests of the states of the Warsaw pact that are involved.

Such a policy of rigidity is bound to lead to a situation in which East Berlin sets itself against the general trend and turns into an island of outmoded Cold War ideas. One day it will simply become too expensive to maintain in the center of Europe a great people splintered against its will and under unnatural tensions.

The Soviet Union, which must think in its capacity as a world power and as a power with responsibility for Germany, will have to coolly assess its interests in a worldwide context. It cannot evade this task. Perhaps it has already begun such an assessment without admitting it. In any case it has, more than once, during the fifty years of its history, revised important aspects of its foreign policy.

When East Berlin complains that we have been trying to isolate it, all I can do is to reaffirm that that is not our intention. On the contrary, we are of the conviction that if there were to be such an isolation, whether caused by others or through East Berlin's own responsibility, the total process of the reduction of tensions in Europe would suffer and be slowed down. It is our desire to move from opposition toward neighborliness between Germans safeguarded by mutual renunciation of force, without which any future merger within a general European order would be unthinkable. But hitherto East Berlin has been doing nothing but setting up obstacles. Accordingly, the German Democratic Republic is not being isolated by us—it is carrying on its own self-isolation.

Our efforts to resume normal relations with all states of Eastern and Southeastern Europe were disturbed primarily by East Berlin. Nevertheless, progress that should not be underestimated can be noted. We have grounds to hope that the possibilities have not been exhausted.

Three conditions for normal relations with the Federal Republic were laid down by the countries of the Warsaw pact:

1 Bonn had to recognize the German Democratic Republic as a state.
2 Bonn had to recognize the demarcation line between the two parts of Germany and the Oder-Neisse line as state boundaries.
3 Bonn had to give up its alleged ambitions for atomic weapons.

Alongside these, a further demand was made: We had to recognize that West Berlin was an autonomous political unit on the territory of the German Democratic Republic.

The policy of the Federal government is such that all these demands could be answered constructively. With good will and with a realistic assessment of the facts and of the significance of the détente for everyone, there need be no obstacle on the path toward a European security system and to a peace order. To be sure, if such conditions are set up in order to evade all conversations, then they can be put forth as insurmountable preliminaries.

1   East Berlin has long been aware of our readiness to negotiate declarations on mutual renunciation of force. In his "Report on the State of the Nation" of March 1968, the Chancellor expressly extended the subjects he had proposed at an earlier stage to include that of a renunciation of force. Further, it was as clearly stated that, if these negotiations produce satisfactory results, the Chancellor would be prepared to meet the Chairman of the East Berlin Council of Ministers.

Renunciation of force means that both sides assure each other not to violate the integrity of the other part, neither from outside nor from within. This is in accordance with the conviction which the responsible political forces in the Federal Republic have always held that the German question must exclusively be solved in peace and freedom.

Ulbricht has said that renunciation of force must be binding under international law. I say that it must of course be as binding as a renunciation of force which we want to agree upon with all Warsaw Pact states. In the case of the German Democratic Republic, however, the obligation would not be one under international law, because contrary to Poland, the Soviet Union and Czechoslovakia, the German Democratic Republic is not and can never become a foreign country for us.

2   The western border of the Polish state was included in our offer to waive all use of force with respect to everyone. Good relations with Poland are particularly important to us and are a cornerstone of our Eastern policy like good

relations with France in the West. Our attitude toward Poland, with its proud past in the history of Europe, is also grounded in the realization that it has suffered much as a result of aggression. Its resolve to live finally within secure borders and its refusal to be a "state on wheels" have our full understanding. A reconciliation with Poland is our moral and political duty. This reconciliation entails not only banishing every notion of force but also ensuring that no seed for a future strife be sown.

A community of interests between the German and the Polish people is recognizable in many areas, including trade, technique, and science but also in questions of the limitation of armaments with the objective of balanced reduction of armaments in Central Europe. In spite of some polemics we believe we can sense the great attention being paid to this question in Warsaw, too. We shall scrutinize very carefully all Polish ideas within this cluster of themes. The impression that in preceding years this was not always the case can be corrected.

The drawing of boundary lines should not stand in the way of the European peace order. If Europe is determined to create a security system and ultimately a stable and just peace order, it cannot be held up by border questions of the past. Perhaps the statements renouncing the use of force that we have already offered can be so formulated and ensured that the present borders of Poland can be recognized for the period for which the Federal Republic can commit itself, that is, until the peace settlement. If that were so the border question, in the interest of both nations, would no longer be an obstacle to a détente or stand in the path of a European peace system. Also, this question could no longer be cited as an obstacle by opponents of a German-Polish accommodation.

3   Since 1954 the Federal Republic has stood alone among the nations with its renunciation of the production of any kind of atomic weapons. In addition, it has subjected itself to international controls over the whole of its atomic industry. We welcome the early conclusion of a universally acceptable non-proliferation treaty which would reduce mankind's fear of an atomic conflict. Such a treaty should be the first step toward the elimination of all atomic weapons and comprehensive disarmament.

The so-called fourth condition can also be overcome. The whole of Berlin—as I have indicated, and as was always respected by the Federal Republic of Germany—has retained a special status ever since 1945, the four-power status, as a consequence of the war and on the basis of international agreements. A special responsibility for West Berlin has grown up on the part of the three Western powers but has not extinguished the four-power status for all Berlin. That means, for instance, that the Soviet Union cannot claim more rights vis-à-vis West Berlin than the three Western powers can vis-à-vis East Berlin.

There has been a variety of points of view revolving around details of this status in the East and the West, as became particularly obvious when the wall was being built in 1961. There is, however, no reason why, if there is good will, it should be impossible to reach practical solutions and improvements. We, in any case, are doing all we can to avoid anything that might lead to the emergence of a dangerous tinder box in Berlin. Consequently we have not touched the status of West Berlin, and so we find ourselves in thoroughgoing accord with the three Western protective powers in the city. The mere fact that the Soviet Union, too, has down to the most recent period repeatedly proclaimed its interest in Berlin and has recognized, at least in principle, a special status for East Berlin, shows that the contradictions here cannot extend so deep that a détente must come to grief on them. If, nevertheless, the specially rigid forces within the leadership of the GDR were to attempt to change the status of Berlin unilaterally, they would jeopardize all endeavors on behalf of the peace in Europe. The Western powers would feel themselves forced to act in harmony with their rights in Berlin and with their obligations vis-à-vis the Berliners. In that case the efforts on behalf of an enduring détente would be destroyed. No one should take such a responsibility on himself.

Our policy in this area, as in the general question of Germany, aims at practical solutions that—without touching the special status of Berlin—would facilitate life in a city, a living organism, that was never before divided, for all those Berliners who had done nothing to bring that division about. Here there exists a special German responsibility vis-à-vis the German city of Berlin. The Soviet Union, too, is aware of this responsibility and at the same time realizes that we have no intention of acting in place of the Western powers.

Summing up, it may be said that in all three domains we have taken the first steps in a new Eastern policy. The way will be laborious. According to our view it leads from the agreed-upon renunciation of force by way of a guaranteed, European security system—in which the two world powers participate—to a solid and just peace order for this continent and with that a solution, also, of all German questions in concert with the Germans themselves and with their neighbors.

The way will also be long. This should not be surprising. Many difficulties have been and are being accumulated. Perhaps too little was done to clear them away. We wish to take this long and difficult road together with all others who are striving for détente and a peace order, especially with the powers that carry the responsibilty for Central Europe and the European states whose future depends on the creation of that peace order.

It is only on this road that Europe will find peace and tranquillity, and the fate of the world cannot be separated from that of Europe. Time is pressing. Even now we sense distinctly the social and economic tensions in broad areas of Asia, Africa, and Latin America that are producing effects in areas not directly affected.

A catastrophe can be avoided only if the full strength of the industrial nations stretching from North America over Europe as far as Japan are concentrated in the service of this grandiose task and are not squandered in a sterile and dangerous conflict. It is here that the truly creative tasks of this epoch lie. In this, the last third of the twentieth century, which we have already entered, it will be decided whether our nations remain so enthralled by the past that they will lose the future altogether or whether they will be able to direct their gaze forward in order to master the future.

15

SAFETY FIRST

Our foreign policy is conceived as a consistent peace policy, a policy by which we mean to eliminate political tensions and curb competitive arming. We are committed to cooperate in proposals for armaments control, reduction and disarmament. On December 6 and 7, 1967, our defense policy was debated in the Federal parliament. In the course of the debate the connection with general foreign policy became apparent and security policy was discussed under its two aspects: defense capability and readiness to cooperate in disarmament. As far as I was concerned, two questions in the debate had priority. First, what has the Federal government done to promote suggestions for the control of armaments and the reduction of armaments? Second, what is it doing in order to come closer to a European peace order and to smooth the path toward it?

As has been seen, the renunciation of force has become the cornerstone of our policy on Europe and the East. We have stated in precise terms our readiness to formulate in a binding way a renunciation of the use of force and of the threat of force vis-à-vis all Eastern European partners.

In the preparatory treatment of this theme we not only have come up against mistrust and polemical imputations, but also have been able to perceive an objective interest in some places. The attitudes of the Soviet government and discussions with it have, it goes without saying, a special weight in all this. Such discussions would have to take place in a confidential manner in accordance with the intent and understanding of both sides. Rapid results cannot be expected. But everyone ought to realize that there will be no lack of good will on our side.

Consultations were held with our allies—within the framework of the Western European Union and NATO—during 1967, concerning the questions of a regional European control of armaments and the reduction of armaments. I have elsewhere referred to the findings of the Council of NATO of December 1967. We wish to collaborate actively in the process of bilateral and multilateral consultations with our allies, with the aim of elaborating specific ideas concerning an offer to the countries of the Warsaw pact.

In order to assume an active role we must carry on our own preliminary study of the problems involved in a balanced reduction of armed forces in East and West, especially of the foreign troops in both parts of Germany. We have such preliminary studies at our disposal, but I am certain that we shall have to give still more weight to these problems—and beyond them to what people have begun to call "peace research"—and that we will have to invest more in them, intellectually and in terms of personnel and organization.

In our policy of détente and of the consolidation of the peace we have been able to count on a high measure of agreement with our allies. That agreement has become clearly apparent in our regular consultations with our French neighbors, as well as with the governments of Great Britain, Italy, and other European countries. It must be made equally clear, to be sure, that the concrete political concert between the Western allies and within the Atlantic alliance still leaves something to be desired. I myself have come out with some vigor for stronger coordination and consultation and was therefore somewhat startled when at the beginning of 1968 it was rumored—with a reference to "Washington circles"—that we were for unilateral actions.

The continued existence of the alliance, its effectiveness, and its further development are necessary from the point of view of a European peace order. There is a good deal of evidence, I am convinced, that an effective European security system could, on a short-range view, be sensibly based only on agreements involving the two alliances, which would go on existing.

The discussions within NATO, in the framework of the so-called Harmel studies, took as their starting point the necessity of a dual foundation for security: appropriate unilateral preventatives for deterrence and defense and realistic measures, free of illusions, to reciprocally control armaments and disarmament. In the so-called negotiations of the three with the United States and Great Britain at the beginning of 1967, we said that we would agree to some cutbacks and troop rotations out of our conviction that our security would not thereby be jeopardized. This is self-evident as nobody would agree to something knowing that his security would be thereby jeopardized. All knowledgeable people realize that, even independent of the focal question of general security, the military presence of each side as well as certain components of it are important factors today. In any case, the reproach that can still be heard in the East to the effect that rearming is going from the West to the East now makes a particularly implausible impression. After all, the Soviet Union, Poland, and the German Democratic Republic have just recently increased their defense budgets considerably. It will be interesting to see whether the de facto though limited changes of the available forces in Western Europe will find an echo within the Soviet sphere of interests or not. A constructive attitude would create an opportunity to promote the détente further even though it might be by only a modest amount. Indifference or deafness shown by the power center of the East can hamper or halt the endeavors for a détente and the real though limited chances of détente. That is the situation.

It is of great importance for our foreign policy that our contribution to defense (in the form of the Federal army, the Bundeswehr) correspond to the obligations that have been assumed.

I think it appropriate to say a word here concerning the Bundeswehr. I know things are not easy for it. I am familiar with the objective difficulties of defining a clear defense mission in a constantly changing world situation. The overcoming of this difficulty and of others is not made any easier by the continuing burden of the past on the position of soldiers in our present-day society. It may be said that after the horrors of our recent history this is no cause for wonder. Nevertheless, I believe that it is time, twenty-four years after the end of the war, to strive for the right sense of proportion here too.

In the bitter years that followed 1945 there was not only the allied order to demilitarize Germany; even without that there were some who had vowed never to bear arms again. The attitude summed up as "Leave me out" never convinced me; yet if it was an error, it was an honorable one. Events have proceeded further, faster, and differently than most people could have foreseen. It is simply not accurate to go on speaking now of the dangers of German militarism, but we know that our country must be capable of standing up for its own defense in this uncertain world. We also know

that the Bundeswehr is the instrument created for and suited
to the purpose. It has put its growing pains behind it, but it
has still not rid itself of some other difficulties.

We are faced with many still unsolved tasks. One of these
tasks consists of reducing the mistrust of us abroad. Another
is to resist energetically the tendency of every army to become a state within the state. A third is to provide the social
equivalent, by means of a healthy historical continuity and
a just assessment of values, for those demands that developed
defense technology imposes on the soldiers. I assign a high
priority to this task, for we require an army whose inner
strength corresponds to its outer effectiveness. In 1967, there
was a debate about the federal armed forces which was
brought about by the strained budget and efforts to offset
the foreign exchange cost arising out of the stationing of
American forces in the Federal Republic. It was no accident
that this debate turned into a discussion of the structure of
the federal armed forces and the necessity of a reform.

The federal armed forces are not an end in themselves.
They are an indispensable instrument of our defense within
the Alliance. Talking about a reform of the Alliance necessarily raises the question of what mission the federal armed
forces have to fulfill. The Federal government did not yet
possess the factual data required to answer that question.
These decisions will also have an important political impact.

We can only hope that in the future it will be possible
to evenly reduce the strengths of others as well as of ourselves.

The Franco-German talks on the security problems of the
1970s will not, on our side, be conducted on the assumption that because of a threatening collapse of NATO we
shall find ourselves in a state of unsecured isolation. We are
concerned with an exchange of views between the two sides,

between the French and German governments. And we expect to arrive at a long-term view covering all of Europe. We
are convinced, however, of the continued existence and development of the Atlantic alliance and its ability to contribute to the process of the consolidation of peace. We also
take it for granted that the treaty I signed in December 1966
will also prove effective. We look upon this treaty, involving
the status of the French troops in the Federal Republic of
Germany, in the context of the agreements between the
French chief of the general staff and the commander-in-
chief of NATO in Europe.

For the future, it would scarcely be endurable if our allies
substantially reduced their military presence on the Continent and then took the view one day that the Bundeswehr
was too big. That means that in all future considerations the
over-all balance of the Western alliance must be a criterion.
In any case we shall strive for this with vigor.

As for the worldwide measures for the limitation on
atomic and conventional armaments, the non-proliferation
treaty was in the center of international interest in 1967.
Other suggestions were not desired. They might have even
been looked upon as a hindrance to the efforts on behalf of
the non-proliferation treaty, after a resolution of the General
Assembly of the United Nations of November 7, 1966, had
forbidden such hindrance. I shall have something to say
concerning the attitude of the Federal government with respect to a non-proliferation treaty. Here I should like to
mention only that in a memorandum of April 7, 1967, we
declared ourselves to be for the linking of such a treaty with
more extensive measures for the limitation of armaments. In
this we brought up once again the idea of a complete cessation of all atomic tests. The previous German suggestion
to cut down, in stages and under effective controls, nuclear

weapons throughout Europe while preserving the relationship of forces should also be recalled here once again.
Though we ourselves are not members of the Geneva Disarmament Conference, we played a not insubstantial role in
influencing the draft of a non-proliferation treaty.

With my responsibility as Federal Foreign Minister I
must emphasize here the fourfold self-limitation of the
Federal Republic of Germany in the nuclear domain:

Renunciation of the production of atomic weapons
Renunciation of control of atomic explosive devices
Recognition of Euratom to control civilian uses of atomic
    energy
Support of the principle of the nonproliferation of nuclear
    weapons

A European peace order must be conceived with the
awareness that it is not enough to reduce the massing of
military power; what is at issue beyond that is the reduction
of political tensions, the accommodation of interests, the
harmony of nations, and the cooperation of states so that
solid foundations may be laid for a healthy European future.
But to attain all this one must make a beginning by blunting
the military confrontation, and while preserving the security
of the European nations and states, one must mutually reduce
armaments and come to agree on control measures. Here I
should like to recall the German suggestion for the exchange
of observers of military maneuvers on the basis of bilateral
agreements.

It would not, as we know, be realistic to expect a complete solution of European problems either today or in the
immediate future. It therefore is not very useful now to
pursue the idea of a European security conference. One
day there surely will also be a conference on the questions of

European security and of the consolidation of the peace. But it must of course be prepared. The times must be ripe.

Meanwhile we shall see to it that in the alliance—that is, in an alliance that includes its American pillar—there is discussion as to what European security and a European peace order should be like. This can then no longer be a matter for mere academic discussion. Our people, just like the nations of all Europe, would like to know what the plan for building the joint European edifice is going to look like.

In East Berlin it is considered offensive when we say that a just and enduring solution of the German question must also be found within the framework of a European peace order. This position is said to be a proof that we would like to change existing conditions, a reprehensible goal, it is said, that conflicts with the consolidation of peace. Once again I ask what it means to wish to change. Is it not true that all those who have serious intentions toward peace and toward Europe must be ready to try to change a few things for the better? All those who are striving toward this goal, after all, wish to replace a doubtful security system by a firm one. They want to replace mistrust by cooperation. They want to end the division of Europe. A renunciation of force, including respect for the borders now laid down in Europe, does not, after all, mean that everything can remain exactly as it is today. Not only is the exaggerated military confrontation in the heart of this continent and on German territory unreasonable, but the wall in Berlin and the death strip across Germany are unreasonable, against nature, and against history.

No one for whom the rights recorded in the charter of the United Nations means something and who takes to heart a peaceful and prosperous future for Europe should be confused as to the necessity of changing something by means of agreements, by means of the accommodation of interests. This holds true for the situation in the other part of Germany. It holds true for the relationship between the German territories and the people living in them. It holds true for the goal of a peace order that must allow the German people some hope for achieving national unity by peaceful means. This does not detract from the intra-German renunciation of force but makes it honest. It puts into proper focus the suggestions of the Federal Chancellor in his letters to East Berlin, which are aimed at making the life of our countrymen and the relationship between the two socio-political orders on German soil more acceptable and more peaceful.

In order to help organize the peace we must recognize responsibility for the Western European communities as well as for Europe as a whole. Out of bitter experience and sincere conviction we want to contribute to overcoming fear and mistrust on our continent. We want to do everything so that Europe can grow together in peaceful, constructive cooperation in such a way that it not only does justice to the welfare of its peoples but also can serve the peace of the world.

It must be manifest to our partners that we clearly agree with the policy we have helped to formulate within the Atlantic alliance, and we stick to that policy.

It must be clear to the government of the Soviet Union and to our neighbors in the East that our defense policy does not contradict our striving toward a détente but is subordinated to it.

Our closest European partners must know that we are in earnest when we seek joint replies to the question of the long-term possibilities of European cooperation.

Our own people must know that we do not intend to be the victims of blind chance or a football for the interests of others; on the contrary, we want to safeguard the security of everyone in concert with our friends and allies. We want to work together with them and with complete frankness toward them—as well as with those others without whom there can be no solution—on opening up the path toward the reduction of tensions and armaments and toward an enduring European peace order.

Robert McNamara, a man who organized the defense of the United States in the 1960s (and whose immense abilities, now that he is president of the World Bank, can also serve the underdeveloped countries), once said that in year 22 of the atomic age the world needs no new arms race. What the world needs in this year 22 of the atomic age is—as he said, and I agree with him—a new race of reason. I can think of no better formula for our policy.

16

"DÉTENTE"
IS NO CATCHWORD

We are not concerned with general confessions; we are concerned with our own German contributions to détente, disarmament, and the consolidation of the peace.

The idea of general disarmament is no novelty. From being a component of historical utopias it has turned into a postulate of practical politics. Nevertheless, to this day things have scarcely advanced even to the point of beginning a freely agreed-on disarmament. It has become clearer and clearer that the reduction of military strength—beyond some modest measures—cannot be attained independent of a reduction of political tensions and cannot in isolation lead to a secure peace.

Tensions are the expression of conflicts of interest. All peace policies must concentrate on the accommodation of conflicting interests and on the elimination of the tensions bound up with them. Thus, the much-used leitmotiv of the present day is "détente." It is worth making the conception of détente precise so that it does not degenerate into a meaningless or misused magical formula.

Although the confrontation of the world powers in Europe has been lessened, as long as the interests of the United States and of the Soviet Union remain unchanged in Europe, a détente will not automatically be produced. If the importance of the European arena is temporarily overshadowed by other global obligations and in consequence the wish for the maintenance of the equilibrium that has been painfully reached here comes to the fore, this will not mean that the specific problems of Europe will be more easily soluble. That is the dilemma we live in. The milder climate of détente is still deceptive and no more than a forerunner of what is to come.

Nevertheless, it is surely right to say that an enduring accommodation of interests between America and the Soviet Union will be indispensable for a general European détente. Such an accommodation is feared by many who think it would be made at the expense of Europe. The two parts of Europe could hardly enter upon a détente against the will of their leading powers, but it is nowhere written that the leading powers, for their part, can, with impunity, disregard European interests. Such a short-sighted policy would not lead to any enduring results.

The European détente will become more tangible if the governments in the East and West learn, from relations that have been made elastic and freed of mistrust, to give priority to their own national and collective European interests as against the sterile formulas of thinking based on blocs. A beginning can very well be made by the reduction of mistrust and the improvement of relations in Europe before the world powers come any closer to a global accommodation.

It is just such an improvement that we are striving for and that many others are equally ready to attempt. Communication between different political and social systems has become possible. We have contributed to a situation in which communications will not be broken off and reason will not again be overshadowed by the doctrinaire rigidity of the Cold War.

In January 1967, before the Consultative Assembly of the Council of Europe in Strasbourg, I made the point that the European nations and states were scarcely capable of achieving a radical improvement of the East-West relationship if the United States and the Soviet Union did not also shift over to this course on a world political scale. Nevertheless, what the European nations and states undertake toward this goal does not have a merely complementary effect. On the scale of world politics it has a quality of its own.

While Western Europe is still preoccupied by the problems of organizing itself, the beginning of a general European community of interests is looming up. It is more than the joint determination to prevent a suicidal war. It expresses itself in practical collaboration. In certain areas and between different partners in Eastern and Western Europe an accommodation of interests is being probed. It is the task of a European policy of détente to extend this still limited area. Practical successes can set in motion developments that will also make possible one day an accommodation of interests in those domains in which it can still not be attained today.

At the same time, it should be soberly recognized that the policy of détente is not in itself the goal. In Strasbourg I explained this as follows:

1 "Détente" is not a magic word. The conception itself will not bring about the disappearance of the tensions and contradictions between East and West. The policy of détente is a policy of accommodation of conflicting aims and interests.

2 Détente is not a goal in itself. It is meant to make

possible an accommodation of interests that will create the foundations of an enduring European peace order. A policy of détente is no capitulation and no flight from reality but is the attempt to gain more and more areas for cooperation.

3 Détente is a comprehensive program. Of course, not all problems can be solved in a single action. One must start where a beginning can be made; one must content oneself with small steps where larger ones are premature. But all this must constantly be in the perspective of wider solutions.

If the government of the Soviet Union and of some of its allies expect us to fulfill unacceptable demands, they speculate on the impossibility of dealing with certain difficulties in the West. That is why it was so important for the Federal government to achieve a constructive clarification of its relations with the Western partners.

What we have in mind is not some nebulous talk about détente, but a realistic program to overcome the East-West confrontation. It includes what we recommended since the formation of the new Federal government, i.e., to consolidate peace through inter-European normalization and conciliation in order to move toward a solution of the German problems within that very framework. This was a starting point for reactivating Franco-German cooperation. It also provided additional common interests with Britain.

The experience and the convictions of my own party, the initiatives and recommendations that the German Social Democrats had been striving for while in opposition, have made their way into official German policy. My efforts for many years as mayor of Berlin, not only against the rigidity of East Berlin but also against some misunderstand-

G

ing in West Germany, have become an element of German policy. What was still the center of a violent dispute when it was being elaborated at the Social Democratic Party convention in Dortmund at the beginning of June 1966 was absorbed into a joint government program by the end of that year. Our ideas on European security and of a European peace order have become components of official policy. For the first time a government statement asked what contribution Germany can make in order not only to maintain the peace but to make it more secure. It is surely no exaggeration to call this a clear change.

It would be premature to present any plan in detail. Nevertheless, I shall attempt to mention a number of principles that in my opinion might lay the groundwork for a European peace order:

> The peace order would have to take into account the fact that different kinds of political, social, and economic systems exist in European countries and that the individual states have sovereign authority in these areas.

> It would have to be ensured that all European states would renounce the use and threat of force, as well as any form of intervention in the internal affairs of other states.

> The relations between the European states would have to be guided beyond all this, by the principles of the charter of the United Nations.

> The freedom of transit and the free exchange of information in Europe would have to be extended as far as possible.

> The NATO states would have to be certain that the peace order would safeguard them what is referred to in the NATO treaty as the "freedom, common heritage and civilization of their peoples, founded on the principles of democracy, individual liberty and the rule of law."

The European states as a whole would have to be able to depend on an effective system for the security of one and all. Such a system of European security would have to be participated in by the United States as well as the Soviet Union. It should result from agreements related to the alliances which, to begin with, would continue to exist.. The German question would have to be solved.

The allies will have to strive, with a purposeful, patient, and undramatic policy, to persuade the Soviet and East European governments that the alternative implied by an enduring peace order is more attractive politically and economically for both sides than the present-day status of Europe. It would be unpolitical—because unrealistic—to press for the entire range of the preconditions between East and West for a European peace order at the same time and with the same energy. Priorities must be set up; the most difficult points being at first put aside. They can be brought up for conversation with greater prospects of success when there is a certain fund of joint regulations on hand and a *modus vivendi* that will not oblige either side to surrender its basic positions and that will have relieved the mistrust on both sides.

The road to a European security system and beyond that to a European peace order can, in fact, be made passable only if the military confrontation, as it exists above all within Germany, is reduced and ultimately overcome. To this end what is needed is the East's readiness to seek security more and more in cooperation between West and East and not in the maintenance of a massive confrontation.

Measures for arms limitations and for disarmament have been suggested by both sides. Insofar as they do not upset the balance of forces they might be implemented by express agreements or, first of all, before the agreements are made, by a tacit understanding and by appropriate mutual action.

A beginning should be made with a balanced reduction of the foreign troops stationed in both parts of Germany. In the East's suggestions, too, this seems to be looked upon as a starting point for the indispensable cooperation between both sides. This measure would also make a direct contribution toward an improvement of the general political climate in Central Europe and work against the hardening of the division. The military consequences, especially the demand for evenly balanced reduction, are being scrutinized at present by the Atlantic alliance, so that a realistic offer at a given time can be made to the Soviet Union and its allies.

In a later phase the balanced reduction should affect those combat forces within their own national borders in Central Europe. With this a reduction of the Bundeswehr could also be discussed. If ever a substantial reduction of the foreign combat forces in both parts of Germany takes place, these forces on both sides can and must also be involved, in order to maintain the proportions and to make possible further advances.

Similar considerations hold true for atomic weapons. Insofar as, due to their deployment, type, and purpose, they are an integral element of the combat forces in Europe, they will sooner or later have to be drawn into any balanced reduction of those forces. This does not exclude dealing with the atomic weapons stationed in Europe as a special element, in the general framework of a reduction of the military confrontation, as long as the balance of forces is preserved. Suggestions aimed at this have been proposed on both the German and the Polish side.

Of a different nature are such measures that, while not directly eliminating the confrontation, soften it and which facilitate direct measures or make them possible at all. In this domain the Atlantic alliance is studying, among other things, suggestions for the establishment of fixed or mobile posts for the observation of terrain on both sides of the demarcation line, for the formation of special military missions, and for the exchange of observers of maneuvers.

I am well aware that none of these steps toward a European security system can be taken from one day to the next. They require a painstaking canvassing of opinion within the alliance and—quite apart from a more favorable constellation for both world powers—undoubtedly long-drawn-out contacts with the Soviet Union and its allies. But one thing that could be undertaken immediately is the renunciation by all parties of the use or threat of force in mutual relations. Opinions may vary concerning the ways and means in which this renunciation is to be accomplished. What is decisive is that the already existing obligation to a renunciation of force between the partners of the two European alliances be confirmed without reservation and at the same time be applied to the problems of the East-West relationship in Europe without prejudicing the solution of those problems. In this way the renunciation of force would become the starting point and the framework for the gradual construction of a security system and—beyond that—of an enduring European peace order.

17

A FOCAL
QUESTION: THE
CONTROL OF THE ATOM

The efforts made since the end of World War II to subject
atomic energy to international controls have come to nothing. Instead we have seen a nuclear race begun between the
United States and the Soviet Union; Great Britain, France,
and the People's Republic of China have also produced and
tested nuclear weapons. In the disarmament negotiations of
the United Nations the conviction prevailed that the spread
of nuclear weapons could best be stopped by a treaty of
universal prohibition.

Since the unanimously adopted Irish resolution of December 4, 1961, the General Assembly of the United Nations has passed further resolutions calling for the urgent
conclusion of a non-proliferation treaty. Of special note in
this connection is Resolution 2028 of November 23, 1965,
because it set up special principles for the content of the
treaty and emphasized more strongly than before the obligations of the atomic powers.

The disarmament conference of the eighteen powers in
Geneva, with its efforts on behalf of general and complete
disarmament, ended in a blind alley. For years it occupied
itself with the problem of nonproliferation, without any

sign of a rapprochement between the divergent points of view. The Soviet Union and other Communist states kept bringing up the issue of the collective defense of the Western alliance. Bilateral conversations between the United States and the Soviet Union remained fruitless for years. During the General Assembly of the United Nations in the autumn of 1966, however, representatives of these two world powers arrived at a nonobligatory agreement concerning certain formulations for a treaty of nonproliferation.

For the first time the draft treaty presented us with the problem of coming to grips politically with scientific and technological knowledge that can no longer be eliminated from the world. The aid and counsel of science are indispensable for politics; but the primacy of political decision must now be asserted in a rather new and unfamiliar domain. Politics leans on the auxiliary partnership of science, but the responsibility of the final decision—and also of important decisions on details—cannot be taken away from the political leadership.

When the Federal government had occasion, at the beginning of 1967, to express itself on the initial results of the American-Soviet understanding, it pointed out that the promotion of a non-proliferation treaty was a principle of German policy.

As early as 1954 the Federal Republic of Germany, when it became a member of the Western European Union and the North Atlantic pact, renounced the production of nuclear, biological, and chemical weapons and subjected itself to international controls. We would have welcomed other states entering upon similar restrictions and thus reducing for themselves the dangers arising out of the spread of atomic weapons. The Federal Republic of Germany ratified the treaty of August 5, 1963, banning atomic tests. Beyond that the Federal government has repeatedly renounced national control over nuclear weapons. It takes as its own the content of the resolutions in which the United Nations has come out for the speedy conclusion of a non-proliferation treaty.

The consultations that we have been carrying on since the middle of December 1966, primarily with Washington, made it clear that the partial draft provided for at the time required changes and additions. We attempted to set up standards by which we could assess a universal treaty banning proliferation. There were essentially four clusters of questions involved here:

1 The unimpeded utilization of nuclear energy for peaceful purposes
2 A clear connection with general disarmament
3 The guaranteeing of security
4 No diminution of regional—and in our case European— efforts for unification

These four clusters of questions gave rise to numerous individual questions that were carefully scrutinized, with the assistance, also, of scientists. It turned out that in none of these clusters of questions were there any interests at stake that touched the Federal Republic of Germany alone and no other state. The Federal Republic was and is, as far as its interests are concerned, very largely in harmony with the other civil nuclear states—in some areas, too, with those that do not belong to any defense alliance.

It lies in the nature of things that the civil nuclear states consulted with each other in order to determine what judgment they should arrive at with respect to the effects of such a treaty on their given national and regional interests and to what extent those interests were in harmony with those of others. This is in the nature of things because in this connection the civil nuclear states constitute the genuine counterpart to the nuclear weapon states. In the circle of the civil nuclear states some are secured by alliances, others are not. Some are members of the disarmament conference in Geneva, others are not.

These conversations have made it clear that the Federal Republic of Germany does not stand alone. We were able to find a great degree of accord on the assessment of the essential aspects of the problem of nonproliferation. During the negotiations, which went on for months, we found a great deal of understanding for our views with our American allies. On a number of questions our consultations with the United States were brought to a positive end.

The unimpeded civil utilization of the atom is a vital interest not only for us in the Federal Republic. The development of nuclear industry for peaceful purposes will go on progressing. The provision of the world with atomic energy will increase. Reactors used for such purposes also produce plutonium, which can also be applied to the production of arms. With the spread of nuclear technology not only will the number of civil atomic powers increase, but inevitably, also, the number of states that will dispose of the objective capacity to produce atomic arms. It is a duty of our generation to stop the military abuse of atomic energy and to promote its peaceful utilization.

The Federal Republic of Germany is ready to support anything that will stop such abuse. It is not ready to accept anything that will hamper the peaceful utilization of the atom, on which the future of the Federal Republic of Germany as a modern industrial state is decisively dependent.

G*

Also, what the Federal Republic can accomplish on behalf of the peaceful progress of mankind depends upon the peaceful use of the atom.

German scientists are known to be working on the development of the second generation of reactors, the so-called fast breeders, and our industry has a good prospect of achieving a high level of accomplishment in this area. We have been striving for an optimal protection of the peaceful utilization of atomic energy and the long-term securing of the supply of atomic fuels by means of binding treaty obligations. Such a treaty most obviously also applies to the exchange of atomic materials, nuclear equipment, and scientific information, as well as to the bilateral and multilateral cooperation of the states with each other or with international organizations in the civil sector. It must apply to research, to industrial activity, and hence also to the export of reactors. We have supported the view that the treaty should even expressly promote the peaceful utilization of atomic energy.

The nuclear weapon states have applied immense funds for the military utilization of atomic energy. Their military experience, to be sure, also spins off valuable knowledge for peaceful purposes. The civil "by-products" of military research are becoming scantier and scantier—so the technical people tell us—insofar as new inventions are concerned. Nevertheless, a monopoly position of the nuclear weapon states emerges for special fissionable material because of the magnitude of the installations and the lower costs of production. Together with others we have come out—not without success—for the sharing by the nonnuclear weapon states of the information and discoveries resulting from the military utilization of atomic energy by the nuclear weapon states.

The projected treaty would prohibit the production of "nuclear weapons and other nuclear explosive devices" by the nonnuclear weapon states, and the passing on of such weapons and devices by the nuclear weapon states. This wording is cogently grounded in the fact that to this day it is impossible to distinguish accurately between military and civil nuclear explosives. For the foreseeable future the application of nuclear explosives to civil purposes will scarcely be of any real importance for Germany. We do, however, welcome the declaration made by the United States, whose research work has not yet been concluded, that it is ready for the establishment of a nuclear explosive service under the supervision of an international authority and regardless of the costs of research and development.

The question of safeguards is very important. Controlled disarmament is a traditional Western demand. It is no novelty for the Federal Republic, which has already subjected itself to international security controls. A consequence of the treaty would be to extend such controls to other states as well.

The application of safeguards must not interfere with economic processes or infringe on industrial production secrets but only counteract the dangers of abuse. What will suffice for this is the control of basic and fissionable material and of the flow of fuels at certain strategic points, if possible by means of automated instruments. Such instruments are not yet in existence. The Federal Republic of Germany will exert all its efforts, in conjunction with its allies and in international organizations, to help develop and establish modern instruments of control. Automation could also make it possible to keep down the costs of a security safeguard system.

Throughout this whole period discussion has revolved

around a draft treaty that does not provide any safeguards in the nuclear weapon states. The Soviet Union has opposed such safeguards on its own terrain. Because of this competitive situation it was of importance when the United States and Great Britain stated at the beginning of December 1967 that they would agree to international safeguards in the civil sectors of their atomic industry within the framework of a non-proliferation treaty.

The spread of knowledge concerning the application of atomic energy cannot be impeded by any sort of restrictions. The production of the bomb is today not so much a question of knowledge as of political resolve. The civil nuclear states are unquestionably performing a real service in adhering to the projected treaty because its essential interest lies in universal validity. Most of them are ready in principle for this because of their perception that any increase in the number of states with independent disposition of atomic weapons means an increase in the danger confronting mankind. If only one more nuclear power were to emerge, people would be afraid of a chain reaction that would be difficult to control.

That is why the civil nuclear states are prepared to contribute their share. This contribution would have to be balanced by one which only the nuclear weapon states can make. There is not only the danger of horizontal but also of vertical proliferation. Stopping the horizontal extension of atomic weapons would be an important step forward, but it still would not solve the problem of making the peace any more secure. One must therefore expect that the nuclear weapon states, in the interest of balanced obligations of the treaty, accept it as a first step toward more comprehensive solutions. A limited non-proliferation treaty must be a beginning and not an end. For the nuclear weapon states this would mean a renunciation of any further development of more and more dangerous weapons; no further increases in the installations on hand, including the means of delivery; the beginning of a reduction; the cessation of the production of fissionable material for military purposes; and the implementation of a complete test ban.

If the nuclear weapon states are ready for such a step and capable of it, the treaty banning proliferation would be the beginning of a movement of international cooperation for ensuring the peace in the atomic age, the goal of the above-mentioned, almost unanimously adopted, Resolution 2028 of the General Assembly of the United Nations. The expectations encompassed there are the hope of all nations throughout the world.

The genuine concern of the Federal government is shown by its memorandum of April 7, 1967, addressed to the participants of the Geneva disarmament conference and to France, which deals with the theme of disarmament in the context of the discussions concerning a treaty of non-proliferation. In addition to the powers in Geneva, we also brought it to the attention of a number of other governments concerned, the Vatican, the Secretary General of the United Nations, and all the missions accredited to the United Nations. This memorandum says:

The devastating effects of atomic weapons make it incumbent on the governments of the world not only to put an end to a nuclear arms race; the interest of mankind demands that nuclear disarmament be initiated. It is only in this way that an international peace order can be created that will vouchsafe to all nations, great and small alike, a prosperous evolution in freedom, independence, and dignity. Germany is resolved to go on working toward this goal together with other countries. The disarmament negotiations of the great nuclear powers have, while achieving some partial successes in the control of armaments, still by no means put a stop to the nuclear arms race. The necessity of genuine disarmament remains all the more pressing. An international agreement on the non-proliferation of nuclear weapons might prove to be a preliminary stage in an effective consolidation of the peace if it is followed by measures of disarmament.

It would have been unrealistic to suggest a special agreement for a general prohibition of the production of atomic weapons and a step-by-step destruction of the atomic arsenal already in existence. It was and remains impossible to disregard the problems constituted by the nuclear arming of the People's Republic of China. The positive reactions to our memorandum, however, encouraged us to give great emphasis to the connection between non-proliferation and disarmament. And this was also given a certain consideration in the subsequent work on the treaty.

The treaty as submitted to the United Nations General Assembly formulates only what is prohibited: everything else is and remains permitted. Questions of the Western defensive alliance are not dealt with in the text of the treaty, but there are connections, so interpretation plays an important role. We had to be concerned with procuring a maximum of certainty with respect to content and form. On the basis of what we and our other partners in the alliance were assured of on the American side, the non-proliferation treaty will not hamper the internal regulations of the Atlantic alliance. There is a certain difficulty in keeping the door open to future defense possibilities in the Atlantic area as well as in the European area, a matter of concern to the alliance as a whole. We understand our renunciation of national control over nuclear weapons, which is an integral part of our policy, as a German contribution to a détente in Europe, and not as discrimination. The arrangements within NATO, through which the Federal Republic participates politically and militarily in nuclear planning, are not affected by the nonproliferation treaty.

On the Soviet side it was said that the Federal Republic of Germany *must* sign such a treaty. This was neither helpful nor evocative of confidence. We made it clear that, as soon as we possess clear data, we shall decide to the best of our knowledge and conscience. It was just these Soviet reproaches and suspicions that showed the special weight ascribed to the decision of the Federal Republic of Germany and how much store the Soviet Union set by the German signature. Here, in spite of the universal character of the treaty on nonproliferation, we were confronted by a special political problem as between a nuclear weapon state and a nonnuclear weapon state.

The Federal Republic does not carry on a policy of political extortion. We reject any policy of nuclear extortion. The Federal government does not talk with two tongues; what it wants to do is to make a contribution to the détente and to an improvement of relations with the Soviet Union and with the countries of Eastern Europe. If in the final study of the treaty on nonproliferation it comes to a positive conclusion, it will be committed to the same restrictions as all the other signatory states. One might really expect the Soviet Union to be able to assess the positive significance of such a step on the part of the Federal Republic.

A balanced non-proliferation treaty can become a factor that will help to weaken and overcome the conflict between East and West. It is unusual but unavoidable for such constructions between East and West to criss-cross, overlap, or supplement elements of the policy of alliances in East and West. This may be confusing, or at least seem so. There is a good reason to think that we shall witness such developments still more frequently in the future. And we shall see that in both camps, with all the caution nourished by the mistrust that has grown up over the years, there will be an attempt to preserve the balance of power that security is grounded on.

The Federal Republic of Germany will be able to defend its interests in such a development all the better the more actively and positively it participates in it. In this world of ours, which has grown so small, with all its perils, its growing global problems, its challenges to mankind, and the international progress in technology and science, there is no longer the possibility of splendid isolation for any nation or any country. The fate of the nation can no longer be determined within the national framework. Security and progress for the nation require cooperation. Not even the Soviet Union or the United States can cope with isolation. In judging the treaty of nonproliferation one must take these considerations into account, too. What must be decisive is whether or not the treaty promotes détente, the consolidation of peace, and the progress of mankind. The excited reactions of individual German politicians have done no service to objective study but have given rise to mistaken assessments of German policy.

On August 24, 1967, the two copresidents of the Geneva disarmament conference presented identical drafts of a treaty in which, to be sure, a clause on controls was still missing. These drafts contained several regulations that were along the lines of our own considerations. Thus, in a binding regulation of the operative section the right of unhampered development and utilization of atomic energy for peaceful purposes and an exchange of information are guaranteed. In the preamble the principle of the instrumental control of the flow of fissionable material at specific strategic points of the fueling cycle is laid down, a clause that corresponds to a desire expressed primarily by the highly industrialized states. The hitherto customary controls through inspectors are to be replaced as broadly and as quickly as possible by automatic instruments, so that unnecessary controls of the techniques of the nuclear installations become superfluous. The expanded preamble also contains a declaration of intent on the part of the nuclear weapon states to place nuclear explosive devices at the disposal of other states on a non-discriminatory basis and at the lowest cost possible. The idea of the participation in the so-called "by-products" of military research is also expressed in the preamble.

On January 18, 1968, these identical draft treaties—including a clause on safeguards—were presented to the Geneva disarmament conference by the American and Soviet copresidents. The Federal government welcomed their presentation and appreciated the improvements that had been achieved. In the operative section, too, the joint draft now provided that all signatories of the treaty bind themselves to negotiate in good faith concerning measures for nuclear and general limitation of armaments and for disarmament.

Amendments of March 11, 1968, underline the connection between the treaty and disarmament obligations of the nuclear weapon states. The safeguards clause was of special importance for us. It allows for the negotiation of a verification arrangement btween Euratom and the International Atomic Energy Agency (IAEA). The European community would be harmed if that negotiation failed, even more so as France does not intend to join the non-proliferation treaty. Moreover, American interpretations made it clear that the treaty would not hinder a development through which the nuclear defense potential of France or Great Britain or both could one day be integrated into a European Federation.

Some wishes remained open. Thus there is no clause banning nuclear blackmail.

We shall see whether further improvements will be achieved during the discussions in the United Nations General Assembly. We cooperate in these efforts, but there must be no doubt about the spirit of any of our criticism. We are in favor of a non-proliferation of nuclear weapons. We shall not have nor do we want any such weapons. And we do not need any such weapons for the policy for which I stand. Otherwise, our efforts to secure peace and reject force would be incredible. This is the very substance of our policy. If the danger of a nuclear war can be substantially reduced, one must be in favor of it provided that the vital interests of one's nation are safeguarded.

18

MISSION:
SECURITY IN EUROPE

We are for a European security system and for a European peace order built up on it. Both together should put behind them not only the Cold War but also the division of Europe.

Mistrust cannot be suddenly replaced by trust. The first step on the way to a comprehensive understanding between the peoples of Europe must consist of taking away their fear of attacks. Only when the security of all is guaranteed can confidence be consolidated and grow beyond cooperation to friendship. Thus, a security system could provide the atmosphere of understanding in which, as we hope, East and West will one day be able to act in concert.

The hostile confrontation of the two power blocs along the Iron Curtain in the center of Germany cannot be overcome from one day to the next. In the area of security, too, therefore, it is necessary to work stubbornly and patiently toward a change in relationships and to build bridges wherever possible.

When we offered the Soviet Union and the Eastern European states an exchange of bilateral statements renouncing the use of force, not the last thing we wanted was to show that the Federal Republic was striving toward its goals only through the peaceful collaboration of all the European nations involved. For this reason we did not insist on a specific form for the exchange of these declarations. This is to be clarified in the course of negotiations..

Once such a renunciation of force has contributed to an improvement of the atmosphere, then the possibility of further agreements that—at first without any change in both alliances—would promote a rapprochement could be probed. Thus, for instance, the exchange of observers at military maneuvers or of permanent observation posts would communicate a greater feeling of security vis-à-vis surprise attacks. Later, more comprehensive agreements would be conceivable between East and West that could entail a change in the alliances and even one day lead to their replacement.

In the preliminary work for a European security system a starting point might be that the present alliances continue, to begin with, and be interrelated. It is also possible to dissolve the pacts and replace them by something new. There are overwhelming grounds for the idea of starting out from the first "model" whenever this theme becomes a matter of practical politics.

It is a good thing for these questions to be reflected on and debated within the alliance. We have a vital interest in these labors, and we are busy with our own constructive contributions. In order to forestall any misinterpretations I hasten to add that the measures and changes being considered must not imply any sacrifice of security. Further, a European security system cannot be divorced from the rights and duties of the world powers. Again and again since the end of the war the East and West have, in the numerous negotiations concerning the future of Germany, presented suggestions for European security, even though very often with tactical aims and not always in touch with reality.

These have become almost limitless in number and content. They have dealt primarily with the following:

The spatial area encompassed by the security system
The stationing or withdrawal of foreign troops
Limitations on armaments
Replacement of the alliances by security regulations based on treaties
Inspections and guarantees

But agreements between East and West in the area of security will come into being only if they are balanced, that is, if neither side is favored. Here what will primarily have to be taken into consideration is that the reductions of armaments and troop strengths in Europe would give the Soviet Union, because of its geographical proximity, a relative advantage. To compensate for this the West must retain a nuclear and conventional defense posture that excludes any miscalculation as to the readiness of the United States militarily to guarantee the maintenance of the security system.

The Federal government has declared its readiness, not only vis-à-vis France, to discuss without prejudice the security problems of the 1970s. To the Federal Republic of Germany, and not to it alone, it is, however, indispensable for the United States to become the bearer and the coguarantor of any future security system. There can be no functioning security system for Europe without the participation of the United States and the Soviet Union.

After the conclusion of the sought-for rapprochement, an agreement will have to be made for a just European peace order in which the division of Germany can also be overcome. It is to be hoped that the governments of the Soviet Union and of the Eastern European states, taking as their

starting point the real interests of their peoples, will collaborate with us in the establishment of that peace order.
Only in this way can the consequences of the last war be
enduringly eliminated and the European nations find their
way to fruitful cooperation.

Even though the Soviet leadership is manifestly seeking
to avoid international crises in Central Europe, it would still
like to limit the détente in such a way that the status quo
is congealed, the United States is forced out of European
politics, and NATO is dissolved; in that way the Soviet
Union would achieve the position of the premier power in
Europe. Till now the Soviet government seems to have
shown little interest in any détente with the goal of "an
enduring and just peace order in Europe."

It is unlikely that the Soviet Union will attempt to expand
its power to Western Europe by military means as long as
NATO can carry out its defense mission. Nevertheless, there
is a noteworthy discrepancy between Soviet military policy
and the declared peace aims of Soviet foreign policy. At the
conferences of Bucharest (July 1966) and Karlsbad (April
1967) the Soviet Union succeeded in formulating a general
line. Nevertheless, within the Warsaw pact divergent opinions concerning the policy vis-à-vis the West manifested
themselves. The conflict between Moscow and Peking fur-
thered the "polycentric" movement in the Communist camp.
The Soviet Union had to sue for the support of its Eastern
European allies in the clash with China and found itself
obliged to loosen its curb on them. Meanwhile, the situation
has changed again.

The success of the liberal tendencies within the Eastern
European states will also depend on whether they can be per-
suaded by a patient, undramatic policy of the advantages of
cooperation between East and West, without their having

to fear any jeopardy to the system they have developed. It will be particularly important to convince the Soviet Union itself of the advantages of the sought-for European peace order.

Direct negotiations between NATO and the organization of the Warsaw pact seem for the time being to be pointless. Instead, preference will have to be shown to the bilateral exchange of opinions of the NATO partners with the states of the East. However, a multiplicity of conversational contacts must not give rise to the impression that the Western partners can be played off against each other. We therefore support the view within the alliance that a canvassing of views must take place concerning important matters that affect all or a number of partners before they are discussed bilaterally with the states of the East.

The Soviet Union is giving very strong support to the suggestion of convoking a "European security conference." We think the time for such a conference has not yet come; nevertheless, we shall give painstaking scrutiny to all the suggestions made on this point. An East-West conference will be sensible only if it can discuss more than the sanctioning of the status quo. It would have to take up the goal of overcoming the division of Europe and seek first of all a *modus vivendi* between all parties. It must at the very least give the assurance that it will promote the process of détente. Furthermore, its failure might mean a serious drawback.

A militarily balanced, phased reduction of the armed forces on both sides would contribute substantially to the détente and facilitate the solution of the political problems of Europe. We ourselves have made it quite clear that we are for troop reductions if they are undertaken as measures for the control of armaments on both sides and can be made use of for an active policy of détente and for establishing the peace in Europe. Parity in the reduction of troops would improve the political climate in Central Europe and loosen up the status quo, as well as improve the psychological situation of the population in the other part of Germany.

As already indicated, the unilateral troop reductions of the West projected for 1968 have, until now, not moved Moscow to take the path of a reciprocal action. As an advance concession toward the Soviet standard offer of a parallel, equally phased withdrawal of foreign troops from both parts of Germany, this Western action is quite unambiguous. The Soviet Union, by an "appropriate counterconcession," would open the road to more far-reaching troop reductions that would, indeed, then be evenly balanced. A negative reaction of the Soviet Union would have to be assessed as an indication that it desires to gain strategic advantages from any overtures on the part of the West.

In any further stages of a parallel reduction on a reciprocal basis thought must also be taken of the withdrawal of a mixture of combat forces that on the Western side would contain more of an atomic nature and on the Eastern side, to make up for it, more conventionally armed troops. A connection might be made with the suggestion made in the German "peace note" of May 1966 "not to increase any further the number of atomic weapons in Europe but to reduce them in stages." Here there are concrete points of departure for initial steps toward a system of European security. If the Soviet Union wants the Cold War to recede once and for all into history, if it, like ourselves, desires peace and security for all Europe, then concrete results will not be difficult to arrive at.

In an interview with the Polish newspaper *Trybuna Ludu* published on January 7, 1968, Foreign Minister Rapacki cast a glance back at one year of Polish diplomatic activity. Among other things he said that it could be seen that the endeavors on behalf of a genuine, enduring détente, of security and cooperation in Europe were growing in strength. More and more people in the East and West were in accord that what should be striven for as a foundation for European security was the creation of a collective security system that would make possible the elimination of the present-day division of Europe into hostile military groupings.

These realizations and considerations belong to the solid substance of Federal Republic policy. They have found expression not only in government statements, speeches, and interviews but also in practical politics. Within the circle of the allies, as well as in the measures and suggestions touching on the relationship of the Federal Republic of Germany to the East of Europe, the Federal Republic is working toward an enduring and just peace order in Europe by means of the dissolution of the tensions between East and West. There is, to be sure, a decisive difference to be noted: Polish Foreign Minister Rapacki has loaded many preconditions into his suggestions. We do not set any preconditions. We are convinced that objective cooperation and the removal of mistrust, will enable the creation of the prerequisites to make soluble the problems that now still seem insoluble.

At the same time, I should like to keep in view the fact that there are points of contact between the suggestions of the Polish Foreign Minister and our own suggestions. Like the Federal Republic, the Polish government says that it regards the renunciation of the use and threat of force in reciprocal relations and of nonintervention in the internal affairs of others as a foundation—or, as Rapacki said, as a suitable framework—for a gradual construction of general European security. There may be differing views as to the manner in which that renunciation is to be realized, but what is important is—and on this point there do not seem to be any differences of principle between the Polish government and ourselves—that the general renunciation of force to which all concerned are already committed be reiterated and thus brought to bear specifically on the East-West relationship.

Like the Federal government, the Polish government, judging by the remarks of its Foreign Minister, sees in a worldwide treaty banning the proliferation of atomic weapons a means of consolidating the peace in Europe and of facilitating further steps toward a détente.

Similar to the plans that bear his and Gomulka's name, Rapacki has during the past year repeatedly suggested regional agreements for a freezing and subsequent removal of nuclear armament in as large a zone of Europe as possible. The German government has submitted a similar suggestion, that is, the suggestion that atomic weapons, under effective controls, be cut down in stages throughout Europe while the correlation of forces is preserved.

The Polish Foreign Minister reaffirms the necessity of a safeguards system for the supervision of regional accords. In his opinion such supervision would prevent surprise attacks. We share that opinion.

Foreign Minister Rapacki has also suggested that conventional armaments in Europe be lowered parallel with measures in the nuclear field. This suggestion coincides with the endeavors of the Federal Republic to reduce the massive military confrontation in Central Europe by means of a phased and balanced reduction of forces on both sides of the line of demarcation.

The Federal government regards it as realistic to give the theme of the renunciation of force a topical significance. It goes without saying that this need not prevent embarking on considerations that go beyond that on the road to the improvement of European security. I regard it as sensible— here, too, like the Polish Foreign Minister—to recognize the fact that NATO and the Warsaw pact are both reliable instruments of our security today and in the foreseeable future. Their existence need not stop the reduction of armaments.

There is no lack of subjects for an objective conversation. There is, to be sure, an obstacle to it, an artificial obstacle, when maximalist standpoints are adopted. This holds for all parties. Maximalism is an obstacle that should be recognized as such everywhere.

19
PATHS
TO SOLIDARITY

The present-day world is determined quite decisively by the United States and the Soviet Union, the two superpowers. Europe has largely become an object of world politics. There is a line of division running through its center, a symbol of the extent to which the creative energies of this Continent mutually hinder and consume each other.

On the path to a Europe that will once again draw strength, in security and peaceful order, for its own viability, there will be many obstacles to overcome. We shall have to make our way forward step by step with patience if we wish to further reduce the mutual fear of people and of nations.

Although this progress will be possible only very slowly in the field of political relations, of security, and of the differing systems and views of life, there are other areas in which the people of Europe can even now take steps to meet and work together, including economics, science, technology, and culture.

In the industrial societies of our world, in which distances are shrinking and the possibilities of communication are growing, the human being finds himself placed in a sort of international solidarity from which he can remove himself only at the expense of his own welfare, progress, and common sense. In many areas tasks are set for the scientist, technician, and organizer whose solution goes beyond or unendurably burdens the material, financial, and human resources of a nation. The need for cooperation imposed by things on people and vice-versa gives Europe the possibility of finding itself once again.

Even now cooperation across the still existing line of division is possible; up to now it has existed only in fits and starts. Joint projects do not necessarily have to start with space travel, the atomic industry, and electronics, even though they too are on the agenda. The time is not yet ripe for these as long as mistrust and a concern for one's own safety go on existing.

There are, however, areas in which one can imagine joint projects that will not lessen the military equilibrium but instead strengthen reciprocal security. Here I am thinking of a comprehensive general European infrastructure, a system of providing and distributing energy, the joint building up of a modern transport network, and the telecommunications technology. Such an infrastructure extending beyond boundaries would, after all, necessarily facilitate communication and substantially increase commercial exchange, which no one can deny are in the interest of Europe.

The advantages offered by an exchange of the results of scientific research and technical and industrial developments are so obvious that they do not have to be especially emphasized. But for this type of exchange what is needed is a minimal amount of confidence, which is only just beginning to be gradually built up. Here the first task of the policy of peace and detente will be to open the way to progress. Then cooperation will be able to take on many forms, from basic research to the international use of the structural and geographical advantages in locating industries, with the ultimate goal of the complete freedom of movement for people throughout the whole of Europe.

In order to come closer to such developments new organizations would not necessarily have to be created. There are institutions already capable of development, such as the World Trade Council, the United Nations Economic Commission for Europe (ECE), and the General Agreement on Tariffs and Trade (GATT). Also bilateral contacts on both a state and nonstate level can lead further, as has already been shown in individual cases.

The Federal Republic is ready to take this path, which will benefit everyone, in cooperation with its friends. It is existentially dependent on a peaceful development, because of its geographical position and because of the dense intermeshing of its problems with the surrounding world. Even hints of a parallel attitude in East and West would be hailed by us as a preliminary stage for conversations and agreements.

In this connection we should not forget the cultural exchange that could smooth the way for some positive development. All previous experience confirms this. I am of the opinion that cultural policy ought to be one of the supporting pillars of foreign policy, because modern foreign policy must be understood as a unity consisting of all its elements. No one ought to balk at the phrase "cultural policy," for it does not imply any desire to manipulate cultural values for political purposes. This would be a far too narrow interpretation of what policy is. Doubts of this kind must be patiently cleared up precisely in Eastern Europe, although here they exist in some circles primarily because people project conclusions from themselves onto others.

Such misunderstandings have prevented our cultural exchange from meeting with a like response from the countries of Eastern Europe. It is not we who are unreceptive; our efforts in this area are comparable to those of any Western country. Whenever there is a need for cultural accords in order to achieve a greater liberalization we are ready to discuss them at any time. Luckily there still exists a certain fund of common European cultural values, which might become still richer and receive many new impulses if communication were free and untrammeled.

General European cooperation is not an end in itself. The last third of the twentieth century will be determined by new fronts. The opulent "north of the cities" is contrasted increasingly by the impoverished "south of the peasants." The consumer states, for which the management of surplus has become a problem, stand out against the still-unindustrialized part of the world whose efforts, in view of the population explosion and of famine, do not even extend far enough to maintain their low standards.

Dealing with this dichotomy is the great task of mankind and especially of the highly industrialized nations. It can be solved only if great portions of the energies of the nations are not, as they have been hitherto, eaten up in conflict, in the menacing competition of armaments. The scientific, technical, and economic means for the conquest of need are on hand or can be created.

It is here that a historic opportunity presents itself. It is impossible to see what might stop us or others from cooperating closer in this regard with Eastern Europe and the Soviet Union. Joint projects do not merely bring objective advantages but also reduce mistrust and can give rise to demonstrations of good will.

Europe has no time to lose. It should take over a portion of the tasks facing the world. This not only would contribute to the lessening of present-day tensions in a worldwide framework but it would make a decisive contribution to deflecting onto the orderly path of progress the upheavals that otherwise would have tragic consequences for everyone.

20

... AND

THE THIRD WORLD

Anyone who mentions the Third World today instantly evokes the idea of aid for development, which is not popular. The story of the golden bed and other stories have not been forgotten. Anyone who equates the concept of the Third World to the concept of developmental aid—more particularly of its distortion—is thinking incorrectly.

As mayor of Berlin and as the chairman of my party I had occasion to meet with numerous statesmen from Asia and Africa before becoming Foreign Minister. At times I would feel a little ashamed to discover how little I knew of the concerns of those countries and youthful peoples and how much interest for our own problems I was expecting from just these countries.

Every one of these countries has a vote in the United Nations, and its vote is counted there just as carefully as that of the United States or the Soviet Union. We sometimes smile at the throng of young nations and their lack of economic strength, of power, of international weight, and often forget that we are smiling somewhat at ourselves, too. To be sure, it is true that strategic bombers, divisions, and technology count, but the world we want for ourselves must also heed and take seriously countries and nations that are not great powers in the classical sense and that have no prospect of ever becoming that—just like, for example, Germany.

The growing contradictions between the developed and the underdeveloped nations—that is, the contradiction between north and south on our planet—will prevent any frontal collision between the numerous small countries and the few great countries. Nevertheless, it is unmistakable that the nongreat powers to an increasing extent are aware of and, today very largely independent of each other, represent similar interests. The Federal Republic can journey for a considerable stretch of the same road in tandem with a good many of these countries.

Understood precisely, this means that the Federal Republic must develop a world policy, though of course not in the sense of a world power policy; but the natural interests of every state demand that it make its weight effective. The political arena has grown bigger. The Federal Republic, too, must become familiar with the fact that, as Professor von Weizsäcker has expressed it, we are approaching the era of *internal world politics*.

Germany does not have much world political experience. The not always felicitous and never systematic excursions outside the Continent before World War I cannot be described as genuine world politics. In the period between the two wars some people, to be sure, dreamed of reviving the colonial idea, but that remained no more than a dream— luckily for us. Vanquished and divided Germany found itself for the first time confronted by the question of how it intended to determine its position in the concert of a rapidly increasing family of nations: what interests it had to represent as an equal among equals in Asia and Africa, and from what points of view the traditional relations with South America, which at bottom had been determined by culture and economics, had to be reviewed.

It is no reproach, merely a statement of fact, that hitherto this has rarely happened, as is quite natural, because the Federal government was always being confronted by novel decisions that were more urgent or seemed to be. In addition, we also needed time in order to become aware of the breakneck development that, with the birth of the youthful states in Africa and Asia, in its turn diminished the relative weight of Europe—that would have diminished its relative weight even if the two superpowers had not emerged at the same time.

I was thoroughly aware of this need to "catch up" when I took over my present office. A conference in Tokyo of our ambassadors to Asia in April 1967 helped me greatly in understanding the new necessities in detail. By the time this book appears a similar ambassadorial conference will have taken place for Africa in Abidjan, Ivory Coast, and a conference for Latin America will have followed in the autumn of 1968. It will be possible after that to sum up the results.

Independent of such conferences, a number of elements of the world political situation can be tabulated for the Federal Republic:

We are not pursuing a power political role of our own in any continent.

We have an interest in the termination of existing conflicts and in the nonemergence, so far as is possible, of any new conflicts.

Wherever we can work together toward a détente we intend to be ready to cooperate.

We are not delivering any weapons to areas of tension.

In these principles the negative formulations, too, have a positive significance. One of the few good aspects of our legacy from the past is that we do not have to pay off any of the mortgages of being a former colonial power. None of the youthful nations has had to wrest its freedom from Germany. To that extent we do not run into any prejudices but meet a readiness for trust and friendship. That is a fund of capital that the Federal Republic must preserve and can preserve only if it applies its policy of peace and détente also and visibly with respect to other continents.

The world has grown so small today that every conflict, even though it does not attain the scope and the cruelty of the Vietnam war and even if the two superpowers are not directly committed, weighs on the situation in Europe. Every conflict conceals within itself the tendency to maintain or to petrify tension and divisions. Thus, every conflict works against the interests of Europe and of Germany. To that extent we are the natural allies of all those who wish for détente, disarmament, and consolidation of the peace. The more active we are in such questions, the more our voice will find a hearing beyond Europe, too.

Our relationship to the individual states is guided by the principle of nonintervention in their domestic and foreign affairs and by the principle of reciprocity and equality of rights.

It is in the nature of principles to sound general, to find agreement, but not always to be easily carried out. The principles just mentioned above have two effects that in detail do not seem so much a matter of course. Reciprocal respect and nonintervention mean that we must not make our relations with a country dependent on whether its form of government suits us. In most Third World countries there is no parliamentary democracy or anything resembling what we mean by that. The stage of development of these countries very often requires other forms of government. We do not have any political models for export.

What we can do, to the extent that we are asked, is to make our experience available. And that we do gladly. In many countries our social order—despite all the shortcomings we are familiar with—arouses great interest. Our trade unions are sought-after helpmates for the development of many countries.

Every continent and every one of its peoples have a tradition of their own, a history of their own, an experience of their own. For this reason alone it is impossible, or it leads only to unrest, if one wishes to transport automatically anything that has been proved among us here in Germany or elsewhere. All we can do is to transmit our own experience, and we must say to every country in all frankness that it must do the chief part of the work itself; every country, in accordance with its own situation and its own interests, must develop, test out, and fill with life the form peculiar to it with the possibilities at hand. In this there will come about new social forms from which the European or indeed the developed countries in general will be able to benefit later on, for we have no grounds for arrogance. The high state of development of our technique is still no proof, as far as human worth and the coexistence of human beings are concerned, that we cannot learn from other cultures. At the same time we realize that these cultures are ineluctably exposed to the process of technicalization and in this will be obliged to demonstrate the strength of their creative substance.

A further consequence of these principles is that we have no fundamental objection if these countries also develop their commerce and their cultural exchange with the other part of Germany, too—not only out of respect for these countries but also because of our view that more contacts with the outside world and a rising standard of living are in the interests of our countrymen between the Elbe and the Oder. Furthermore, it is not compatible with our national dignity to carry abroad to other continents our internal German disputes and problems, to put it mildly, or to vent them there bureaucratically. Reciprocity and equality of rights do not mean, of course, that the Federal Republic surrenders its own interests. We shall not run after anyone who does not accept our policy of détente, including internal German détente. We are no petitioners. Nor must the Federal Republic allow itself to be blackmailed, either. If a government is of the opinion that it will get a better commodity or better credits in East Berlin, it should do so.

Every country is free to select its own friends. This also applies to the Federal Republic. There is no threat in such an attitude, nor can I see any misfortune if a team of machinists from Madgeburg sets up a well-functioning German installation somewhere in the world.

If we cultivate the friendship of many countries and develop our common interests, the Federal Republic will then find political and moral support whenever it needs it.

There is a third manner by which we can document our friendship with the nations of the Third World. We know today that in a relatively short time we shall be confronted by the problem of combating naked hunger throughout the world. The curve of growth of the areas opened up for cultivation is substantially flatter than the curve designating the growth of population. The "have-nots" against the "haves" was the situation in many European countries during the first industrial revolution, and such tensions, on a world scale, now await us. It makes no difference whether we think of ourselves as the Christian Occident, as a libertarian democracy, or as humanist socialists—the challenge facing us all will put our common ideals to the test.

The tasks arising out of it are titanic. They transcend the forces of every individual nation. This does not mean, to be sure, that the Federal Republic could not make its own contribution to development aid. I see this contribution primarily in an area that will enable these countries to gird themselves against the perils of overpopulation and hunger.

It is not opportunism but the simple truth to say that these tasks of the future can be coped with better by a united Germany, a united Europe, than by a divided one. Europe itself has fallen back and must catch up. There has been as yet no success in convincing the peoples of Asia, Africa, and Latin America that European unification lies in their own direct interest because that is what will release powerful forces.

A Europe grounded in peace and security would be a powerful element of stability. And it is stability that the youthful nations need, that the world needs, so that humanity, which increases daily by the number of inhabitants of a middle-size city, can exist with human dignity. This may sound as though it were a question of some remote prospect, but the lapse of time between the day the first atomic explosion mushroomed up to the skies and the beginning of this year of 1969 is much longer than the lapse of time left to us if we are to save literally many millions of people from death by starvation.

At the beginning of this chapter I recalled that most people think of development aid when the Third World is talked about. As far as the problems of the Third World and the position of the Federal Republic are concerned, development aid is only a single point among many, and not even the essential one.

Perhaps what is necessary is a negative line of demarcation of what development aid is not, or should not be: it should not be charity, not a purchase price for countries or people, not the indispensable fertilizer for mere show-case projects meant to satisfy a desire for prestige. It ought to be aimed at economic utility, as help for the purpose of self-help, with eyes directed at the problems of the next ten to fifteen years. As such it is help for us, too—for our economy, for our exports, for the establishment of markets, for the ensuring of jobs. There is no need for us to be ashamed of speaking these truths aloud.

We should see to it that projects really are of mutual interest. Here the industrial countries have sinned no less than the underdeveloped countries. Every country would like to be independent, but our world—even the most powerful countries—is moving into a situation of constantly growing mutual dependences. Dependence that is not oppressive, in which each individual can develop fully is the goal for the position of the individual in society and of the states in the family of nations.

In the countries of Asia our peace policy has found a positive echo, and many unused possibilities offer themselves for economic cooperation. Strengthened contacts between the economies of Germany and Japan would also benefit regional cooperation in Southeast Asia. For our development policy India, Pakistan, and Indonesia are of special interest because of their size and political importance.

In Asia—though not there alone—there is an impression that export trade is being damaged by the EEC. The dynamics of the Common Market, which lead to increased imports, is overlooked. This factor adds all the greater importance to the demonstration that we champion a liberal course for the EEC, open to the world.

Everywhere in Asia, though with varying intensity, there is interest in cultural relations with Germany, and there have been excellent beginnings toward cooperation in the areas of science and technology. However, we shall be able to perform the numerous economic, cultural, and political tasks lying ahead of us only if our citizens show a clearer recognition of the meaning of Asia for their own interests. We laid all this down at the ambassador's conference in Tokyo and made the additional point that the Federal Republic must lend support where traditional friendship and existing good will come halfway to meet our striving for cooperation, détente, and stabilization.

Of the 122 votes in the United Nations (and in the other international organizations) 39 belong to African states, yet Africa has no more than 10 percent of the world's population. This disproportionate voting strength, but above all, too, our commercial interests, have made it seem necessary for us to be represented almost everywhere by resident ambassadors. Apart from the United Nations, Bonn is the greatest center for ambassadors from black Africa.

Our relations with most of the African states are good; with some of them, very good. For their development they need close cooperation with the industrial nations. The Federal Republic is a sought-after partner, because Germans have a reputation for efficiency and stand less under the suspicion of wishing to meddle than do the former colonial rulers or the Communist countries. An additional link to the eighteen associates of the EEC is taking shape.

Although our policy strives for good partnership, this does not prevent Communist propaganda, especially out of East Berlin, from denigrating us as "neocolonialists" because of our normal relations with South Africa, the Portuguese possessions, and Rhodesia. This relationship has nothing whatever to do with sympathy for racial inequality.

The process of decolonization has been accomplished only in the most recent past and is not yet quite finished. We must expect major convulsions to lie ahead of the continent. It is our task to take care of German interests on the spot even in difficult circumstances, to contribute within the framework of our potentialities to the development and consolidation of the new states, and to further the contact between Africa and Europe, which in the future will be very important for both sides.

In the Middle East, too, we are bound to be concerned with the protection of our economic interests. We likewise have an interest in preventing the security of Europe from being jeopardized by the "southeast flank."

During the Middle East conflict that in June 1967 culminated in an armed clash, we followed a policy of noninterference. This position—propped up on the recommendations of the United Nations—is bound up with the desire for an enduring, just, peaceful solution.

Noninterference does not mean that we could accept a policy aimed at the destruction of the state of Israel; that would be morally reprehensible and would run counter to the properly understood interests of all parties. The restitution payments that were agreed on against the macabre background of the annihilation of millions of Jewish lives have been settled. Today Israel receives economic aid as part of our normal, worldwide programs.

The Arab states have also participated in the German programs, and we are ready for more comprehensive cooperation. Our readiness to give humanitarian aid has been announced, and the Federal government has declared itself ready to make special efforts on behalf of the refugees in the coming years.

In 1965, after the establishment of relations with Israel, nine Arab states broke off diplomatic relations with the Federal Republic. Morocco, Tunisia, and Libya did not join in this measure; Jordan resumed relations in 1967, as did the Republic of South Yemen, established at the beginning of 1968. We have remained present in all capitals and have been able to make various contacts that will serve normalization. This is also to be desired because the cultural bonds that have always existed between the Arab world and Germany can be elaborated and amplified on a friendly basis.

Latin America does not appreciate being drawn into the unnuanced collective concept of "undeveloped countries." And in fact there is a fundamental element in our relationship to most of the countries of Central and South America that arises out of common principles of freedom and human dignity. The Latin American peoples feel themselves to be wholly part of the West. This relationship goes beyond spiritual and cultural connections.

Yet it is precisely on this subcontinent that the question arises as to whether or not the democracies are capable of renovating old structures, of linking together economic growth and social security, and of keeping the banner of progress from falling into the wrong hands.

A number of Latin American governments have begun to tackle the solution of the great economic, sociopolitical, and population problems. German and European policy with respect to Latin America must be aimed at establishing a partnership for progress that will rest on common interests.

German aid beyond the traditionally well-anchored economic and cultural relations can only be modest. It must be embedded in the deepening of political conversations and in the sharing of each other's problems. The feeling of reciprocal dependence, of attachment, and of a common world political responsibility must be strengthened and must prove itself in the chilly air of this era.

21

LESSONS
OF YESTERDAY—
SIGNALS FOR THE FUTURE

In all the ages of human history the idea of eternal peace has been the goal and content of utopias and philosophical systems. The practical results have been rather depressing. But the spiritual energies that were devoted to this ideal have nevertheless not been squandered futilely. Without them there would not be some of the moral principles that in spite of all the tensions in the world have remained alive.

A peace policy in our time must apply itself to the host of problems in the sequence of the realizability of their solutions. It must move on from the simple to the difficult.

This decision in favor of what is realizable is no novelty in the history of peace efforts but comes to light in plans for European unification that can display a history of some six centuries. In spite of all differences they had one objective in common: to set up in Europe an enduring peace order. But they all shared the fate of either remaining no more than drafts or else collapsing in the very first attempt at realization.

Beyond or instead of an immediate regional solution, these efforts tended toward a global peace organization. The League of Nations—with its reasonable and still relevant objectives—was a great hope for many people after World War I. But it was that, unfortunately, only in the preparatory stage. When it came to life, it was incapacitated, by the abstention of America and Soviet Russia and by the exclusion of Germany, from really mastering the problems of Europe and of the world. The idea of international solidarity could not be established. National antagonisms were too strong, and frictions did not allow any space for the beginnings of integration.

The United Nations, too, which was founded at the end of World War II in San Francisco as an optimistic scheme of the victorious powers, is not a full-fledged or perfect representative organ of the nations. Germany is not represented in it, nor the People's Republic of China—Germany because it is divided, China because it is isolated. Nevertheless, the United Nations has a different structure and quality than the League of Nations. It, too, is incapable of eliminating weighty conflicts of interests, and in any "crisis management" success and failure are wholly dependent on whether or not the world powers work together and are capable of uniting from one case to another. But the United Nations has nevertheless established peace in numerous regional conflicts and accomplished a great deal, not only in a humanitarian way but also in concrete international cooperation. This speaks for its usefulness. Beyond that the General Assembly of the United Nations is a mirror of the opinions, hopes and interests, tensions, and conflicts in this world and thus a source of information and inspiration for the foreign policy of many states.

The Federal Republic of Germany does not stand outside the United Nations, though it is not a full member. It belongs to the European Regional Economic Commission of the Economic and Social Council and to all its special and auxiliary

organizations. It is making substantial contributions to all
the important aid and development funds and is invited to
collaborate on specific occasions by the member states and
by the Secretariat. Its permanent presence in New York and
Geneva offers interesting possibilities for diplomatic and
political contacts. The assembly halls and corridors are a
place for encounters not easily duplicated elsewhere.

The United Nations is important for us, too. We must
not, to be sure, expect too much from it in the way of a
cure for the European division and for the establishment
of a general European peace order. This task has been set
for the Europeans and cannot, in any case, be solved by
majority resolutions in the New York palace of glass.

The perniciousness of the European division really does
not need to be demonstrated any further. Power blocs that
have been formed against one another and are more or less
solidly constructed cannot last very long in a narrow space
without lapsing into the dreadful danger of a conflict. That
is the lesson of history. But the two power blocs on European soil have at the same time organized themselves into
two—varying in nature—social orders. In both domains the
bilateral possibilities of conflict have been reduced. This
state of affairs is to be preferred to a balkanization, with all
its incalculable consequences. A collapse of the two alliance
systems without their being replaced by a new order would
not promise a healthy future.

Social orders are not immutable. We are witnessing an
evolution of systems. The gray uniformity of Stalinism
belongs to the past. And the very appearance of even a
reduced threat has been enough to bring some movement
into the Western alliance. It is not simple to distinguish here
between causes and effects. Is the incipient détente the con-

sequence or the cause of the evolution? The fact remains that we are living in an age of transition.

Hardly anyone will be able any longer to contest the fact that the loosening up of the cohesiveness within the blocs has allowed national identities to become more obviously visible again. This development, which in principle is surely to be welcomed, also conceals risks. A new order will only be found if the centrifugal forces do not gain the upper hand and if a joint effort is made to find a solution to the disputed questions.

No one would wish to assert that there are no longer any national conflicts of interest in Europe. In the West such conflicts make European unification more difficult, and in the Mediterranean area they lead to a considerable and perilous insecurity. National questions exist in the East, too. Yet we know that the revival of national passions leads to disaster. That, too, is the lesson of history.

We cannot foresee the evolution of the coming decades. We do not know if the present-day powers will really be able to maintain the existing order in the era to come. But one thing is certain: it would not be good for security and for the consolidation of the peace if future German governments had no other choice than to pursue national ends by national means. It is a commandment of historical common sense to solve the German question—the greatest national problem of present-day Europe—within the framework of a general European peace order in such a way that the right to self-determination is satisfied by it just as well as the legitimate interests of the neighboring states.

Taking as its starting point the right of the nations to self-determination, a European peace order must lead to new forms of an orderly and no longer inflamed coexistence

of nationalities. That holds true for us, too, but we have
learned that for us there is no swift or isolated solution.
Together with France and with our other Western neighbors we are setting about the work of overcoming the abyss
that separates the nations in the East and the West of our
continent and that sunders our own country. Only within
the framework of a progressive European peace order is a
just solution conceivable for our special problems, too.

Our attempts to bring about a détente in the European
situation are still overshadowed by the East-West conflict.
But this conflict has been transformed and will be transformed still further. Some previous prophets of world revolution have also begun to perceive that there are more
important interests and developments than the triumph of
an ideological system. The ideological revolutionary must,
in the age of atomic weapons and space flight, become a
relic of the past. I am therefore convinced that we—as the
result of a process full of contradictions—shall make progress when it is a question of normalizing relations between
the nations and states of Eastern and Western Europe.

Europe will ultimately comprehend that the peoples in
the East and the West share a common destiny beyond everything that divides them. This destiny can be turned to good
only by an enduring peace order. That is the way in which
we intend to work on the construction of the European community and on making a bridge across Europe. Anyone who
sabotages this policy becomes a disturber of the peace. In
the long run disturbers of the peace will prove unable to
maintain themselves in Europe and in the world. Anyone
who pretends that this policy is neo-Nazi, revanchist, and
militaristic is denouncing, with outmoded catchwords, a policy of truthfulness. We have invited statesmen from the
West and the East to come to us, to talk with us, and to form

their own picture of German life. It is not we who are threatening our neighbors with military aggression. We offer them, rather, a mutual renunciation of force. It is not we who vilify everyone who does not share our opinion in everything. We endeavor to argue in an objective way and to put ourselves on good terms with those, too, who think differently.

It is true that the securing of peace and order in Europe is not difficult only because of the existing power relationships. The ideological division is still a reality. But even the ideology of communism is not a canon cast in iron that could survive unchanged for centuries. Today communism, even in its own realm, is anything but a strictly hierarchized and undisputed world religion. It has been transformed, and it will be transformed still further. Transformation happens to be the destiny of systems in this age of ours.

Our own Western social orders are surely not immutable, either. As far as we can foresee—and in accordance with the will of their peoples—they will cling firmly to the idea of democracy. But they will go on constantly developing further; they will have to be open to change and to the new challenges of the surrounding world in order to extend to the limits of the horizons that keep being set further and further away by technology, by the sciences, and by the new industries. The freedom of the individual will soon no longer be a question of a political constitution but an organizational problem of a technicalized environment.

It is too soon to speak of any rapprochement between the two contradictory worlds of ideas. Yet these are developments that I do not consider illusory but ineluctable and that we must prepare ourselves for. The material future of mankind will be molded still more strongly than now by technique and by the natural sciences. There will be little room for ideological dogmas. The socio-organizational problems of the highly industrialized states will grow steadily more similar to each other in the course of technical-scientific progress. That can facilitate the understanding between them and permit them to become more conscious of the common nature of their interests.

For the time being the present offers only scattered signs that make such a development believable. Nevertheless, there appears to be, here and there, a clearer recognition of the vast demands heralding the advent of the future. The states of Eastern Europe are also subject to the urgent priority of solving economic and social problems as rapidly as possible, and such solutions will be possible only in a stable international situation. Greater economic independence must be secured, while at the same time the requisite stability must be still more extensively guaranteed. This is hardly a question of ideology. In the Eastern bloc a system of unity in diversity is growing up—also a sort of equilibrium of interests, which the leaders of the Communist Party of Rumania have formulated as follows: "Diversity constitutes the ineluctable and irreversible framework for the activity of the Communist parties."

Policy in the Communist countries is almost exclusively determined and controlled by the Communist Party. When changes occur, consequently, they are bound to be internal party changes. Indeed, there are signs of them even now, but that does not imply that they mean any democratization in forms we are familiar with. If the Communist parties intend to carry out their role as leaders of the state, they will require, in view of the challenges of the second industrial revolution, a broader social base than in the past. Endeavors to establish such a broader base are unmistakable everywhere in Eastern Europe. The intellectual and technical elite is strengthening its influence. And the campaign for active collaboration in economic and social life is more intensive than hitherto.

If evolution within the Communist realm keeps being determined more and more strongly by objective necessities and by material interests, this can increase the chances of finding a common language for the assessment and accommodation of interests between East and West in Europe.

These lines had long been written when promising developments took place in Czechoslovakia. They were the exclusive merit of those who, in that country, courageously and with a sense of proportion, did what they thought right. They wanted to make Socialism more attractive and to adjust it to the future. They wanted to prove that Socialism and dictatorship were not necessarily synonymous. The conservative forces then tried to reverse the "1968 Prague Spring" by forcible intervention from outside. The Czechoslovak people has met that attempt with an attitude that commands our whole-hearted admiration. We do not know what the outcome of this struggle will be. And we can but wish that our neighbor nation be spared new sufferings. We do, however, know this: The internal process in the CSSR under the leadership of the changing Czechoslovak Communist Party as of now forms an integral part of European history and like anything that happens on this continent will have its effects on the neighbors, all neighbors, of that country.

In East Berlin little internal progress of communism is to be noted. But the intransigent attitude of the German Communists has less to do with ideology than might often be thought. It is the expression of crude self-interest that sees itself threatened by progress. But if the general European interest in an enduring peace order is what puts its stamp on our future, the East, too, will be unable to ignore the fact that a quarter of the German people is not a pledge worth surrendering security and peace for.

And indeed the recognition is growing that the nations of Europe must and will not simply come to terms with being permanently divided by the conflict between East and West. The insight is growing that Europe belongs together not only through its history but also through its destiny. Even fundamental differences of political conviction and of social structure need not hold back the states of Europe— and will not, as experience has already shown, stop them— from working together in areas of common interest for the consolidation of an enduring peace. Ideological group interest and thinking in terms of blocs will have to retreat behind these "new realities," and it will become obvious how much both the national interest of every people and the interest of Europe require organizing peace.

22

PERSONAL
EXPERIENCES

When I took office I had intended to sit at my desk as much as possible and travel as little as possible. In practice this intention proved to be realizable only to a limited degree. Good will alone does not suffice.

Established practice of consultation makes the foreign minister travel a lot. The amount of time, preparation, and personnel involved is not always proportionate to the results. Yet, even if all concerned were aware of that danger and tried to counteract it, a considerable measure of routine would remain unavoidable.

Wherever one wants to press a point and prompt other governments to some particular course of action or hold them back from certain actions, distant trips are often necessary. Jet flight, which has made even the greatest distance shrink to a few hours, theoretically saves us time. Yet this advance has cost us dearly—just because it seems to take so little time one decides on additional lightning trips. Instead of being made freer because of the modern means of communication—not lazier, but freer for reflection, for reading, and for tranquil conversations—they lead to a highly developed form of slavery.

The teletype sees to it that over and above other information there is a scarcely interrupted torrent of information coming into the headquarters of the Ministry for Foreign Affairs. To pick through the abundance, to separate what is essential from what is otherwise also necessary, and to study it is once again a question of the economy of energies. The timetables of government, party, and parliament also press their rights.

In looking back on the period since the formation of the present Federal administration in December 1966, I can perceive that the problem of having time for the important things has become of equal significance alongside all others, including the most important substantive problem. It is only a relative consolation to know that one's colleagues are in the same boat. In any case, it is a sign that governmental procedure is in urgent need of reform.

In this respect, too, we are living in a period of transition. The mechanisms of conducting foreign policy in an age of "world-wide domestic policy" will have to be different from those that have come down to us. We are working, on occasion painfully, with an outmoded range of instruments today, when it is a question of assessing the growing drive toward multilaterality, toward the satisfaction of a hunger for information that scarcely lets up for a single hour, toward the heeding of the desires of a pluralistic society. The provision of additional jobs in the budget is occasionally unavoidable, but it can also mean a postponement of structural decisions.

The word "reform" is—methodologically, in any case— the answer to this problem. I know that a reform, particularly of the Foreign Office and of the Foreign Service, is a task that is difficult and not to be realized speedily. One will have to keep in view the necessary modernization of governmental activity and not pass heedlessly by the experience of other states. I hope that the basic lines of a reform will be worked out among us before the next elections.

This Federal administration set about its task in December 1966 with some elan and much good will. If one recalls the very modest and by no means roseate picture of the situation in which the Federal Republic of Germany found itself at that time with respect to foreign policy, one may surely say without exaggeration that the danger of isolation has been banished. We have gained some more latitude, and we have found out at the same time just how limited it is.

It is a question not only of the restrictions arising out of objective factors. Subjective, internal political factors, too, can be a substantial obstacle to the development of an independent and realistic foreign policy. And indeed, not only traditional, nationalistic, and selfish party influences exercise a retarding effect; there are also obstructions that grow up out of illusions, a flight from reality, and political incomprehension.

It was impossible to bring about the extension of the European communities in *one* new swoop, but it seems certain to me that this theme will no longer be dropped. This single, decisive component of our European policy will make a heavy claim on our activities in the field of foreign policy. And we shall have to accustom ourselves to the idea that on occasion we shall have to waive agreement and ready ourselves for a difficult period.

Nor will the other, the East-West, component of our European policy bring more than partial further advances. For a long time now it has been my view that in the condition of German division time cannot be relied on to work for us. The policy of détente meant casting off some ballast; it made our ship ocean-going, to be sure during a period of ebb tide. But unlike the times of ebb and full tide, in politics the times when the waters will rise again cannot be determined or forecast with any certainty.

Only very few observers were aware that 1967 brought us, after tenacious efforts on our part, an offer of talks from the Soviet Union, the first ones since the resumption of diplomatic relations in 1955. Everyone will understand that the thawing out of congealed and iced-over barriers between the Soviet Union and the Federal Republic of Germany is impossible in a few months. It is obvious that the restoration of friendly relations lies in our interest. No one can doubt that this is impossible without dangers and risks. Anyone who is afraid of these should not speak about Eastern policy. Anyone who underestimates them should be kept away from Eastern policy.

There can be no question of selling out. These silly catchwords create the impression partly that those in charge of German policy have nothing else in mind and partly that there is nothing else. The problem is formulated by the facts: both sides must probe their positions if they are to and wish to collaborate fruitfully with each other. And that is indispensable for the interest of security and of détente in Europe. At the same time, it can even be useful to recall Konrad Adenauer's recipe—the one about installment payments— that in its time was applied by him with some success to the West. We shall be able to apply this profitably to our relations with the East only if we maintain our relationship of friendship and trust with our allies.

In this relationship there is no either-or. Foreign policy is the sum of all factors made to bear fruit in the interest of a country. Nevertheless, I should like to emphasize here once again that friendship with the United States is of vital consequence for us. It is all the more important if we are steering toward a Europe that is to play its own role and serve the peace by its own means.

The distance between today and the year 2000 is shorter

than that between the year 1933 and the present. Yet we realize that the policy of the Federal Republic of Germany is still influenced by the year 1933 more strongly than by the year 2000. That burden and inheritance cannot be simply shed from our internal politics nor even our thinking. In foreign policy our opponents take advantage of the general habit of and the capacity for keeping the past in mind better and for imagining the future with greater difficulty and turn these against us. Our friends as well as our enemies, both inside and outside, must be fully aware of the fact that the problems of tomorrow—the population explosion, the north-south conflict, the revolutions in science and technology—need to be solved today. That is impossible as long as we keep looking backward.

We have entered the last third of this century. German foreign policy must be free for it—or make itself free for it. And by doing that we shall set free additional energies for peace in Europe and the world.

About the Author

World-famous mayor of Berlin: 1957–1966 (he left Germany in 1933 and served in the Norwegian Resistance during World War II), Herr WILLY BRANDT is a key figure in the current German coalition government, which took office in December 1966, holding the offices of Foreign Minister and Vice Chancellor. As leader of the Social Democratic Party, he is a strong contender for the chancellorship of Germany when elections are held in the fall of 1969.